SALT

Servant Approach Leadership Training

SALT Institute
Woodland Park Baptist Church
Chattanooga, Tennessee

Servant
Approach
Leadership
Training

Module 103 Student Manual
Building A Biblical Philosophy of Ministry

SERVANT APPROACH LEADERSHIP TRAINING: Building Biblical Philosophy (revised 2/20/223)

MODULE MATERIALS

You will need to bring this course module and the following materials to every session:
- Notebook paper for taking notes
- Pen or pencil for note taking and filling out forms
- A New American Standard Bible

You will need the following materials to have available for doing your homework and it is optional to bring these to class:
- Colored highlighters or colored pencils (at least six colors)
- ✢Spiros Zodhiates' *Complete Word Study New Testament* from AMG Publishers
- ✢Spiros Zodhiates' *Complete Word Study New Testament Dictionary* from AMG Publishers

In addition, you will need access to the following materials for homework assignments:
- An exhaustive concordance (Strong's, NAS, or computer-based)
- A good Bible dictionary (e.g. Unger's)

No part of this book may be reproduced in any manner without written permission from the publisher.

Scripture taken from the NEW AMERICAN STANDARD BIBLE®, Copyright © 1960,1962,1963,1968,1971,1972,1973,1975,1977,1995 by The Lockman Foundation. Used by permission.

> "When a man is simply told the truth, it remains external to him and he can quite easily forget it. When he is led to discover the truth himself it becomes an integral part of him and he never forgets."
> —William Barclay

MODULE 103 OVERVIEW

MODULE TITLE: PHILOSOPHY OF MINISTRY
MODULE THEME: UNDERSTANDING BIBLICAL MINISTRY
MODULE VERSES: COLOSSIANS 1:25-27

> Of this church I was made a minister according to the stewardship from God bestowed on me for your benefit, that I might fully carry out the preaching of the word of God, that is, the mystery which has been hidden from the past ages and generations; but has now been manifested to His saints, to whom God willed to make known what is the riches of the glory of this mystery among the Gentiles, which is Christ in you, the hope of glory.
> Colossians 1:25-27

SESSIONS

ELIJAH: A CASE STUDY IN RECEIVED MINISTRY	4
BUILDING A BIBLICAL PHILOSOPHY OF MINISTRY	18
PHILOSOPHY OF SERVANT LEADERSHIP	25
JOHN THE BAPTIST HOMEWORK	31
JOHN THE BAPTIST NOTETAKING OUTLINE	35
PHILOSOPHY OF CHURCH GOVERNMENT	38
THE SEVEN PILLARS FOR A BIBLICAL PHILOSOPHY OF MINISTRY	46
PHILOSOPHY OF ORDINATION	51
PHILOSOPHY OF EVANGELISM	56
PHILOSOPHY OF DISCIPLESHIP	61
PHILOSOPHY OF MISSIONS	69
PHILOSOPHY OF CHURCH	78
PHILOSOPHY OF RESTORATION	85
PHILOSOPHY OF WOMEN IN LEADERSHIP	102
PHILOSOPHY OF RETREATS AND CONFERENCES	107
PHILOSOPHY OF BEGINNING A NEW MINISTRY	112
PHILOSOPHY OF BIBLICAL COUNSELING	120
PHILOSOPHY OF CHILDREN'S MINISTRY	128
PHILOSOPHY OF CALLING CHURCH STAFF	136
PHILOSOPHY OF ELDERS AND DEACONS	144
PHILOSOPHY OF EQUIPPING	153
PHILOSOPHY OF STUDENT MINISTRY	158

SERVANT APPROACH LEADERSHIP TRAINING: Building Biblical Philosophy (revised 2/20/223)

Elijah: A Case Study in Received Ministry

Introduction:

Bible Study Segment #1:

Elijah came onto the scene at a critical juncture in Israel's history. Let's go back in time a little bit to present a review of the events that led up to the time of Elijah. Solomon replaced David as king. In his later years Solomon's wives turned his heart away from God, and he *"did what was evil in the sight of the LORD, and did not follow the LORD fully, as David his father had done"* (1 Kings 11:6). As a result, Israel split into two kingdoms. The northern ten tribes followed Jeroboam, Solomon's slave master, and were led into false worship complete with idols, pagan altars, false priests, and even false feasts. The Northern Kingdom languished through a series of wicked kings from Jeroboam to his son, Nadab, who followed in his sinful footsteps (1 Kings 15:26), and then to Baasha who did likewise (15:34). Baasha was succeeded by the drunken king, Elah, who was assassinated by Zimri, his commander. Zimri's reign lasted only seven days, but he is characterized as walking in the sinful ways of Jeroboam (16:19). Zimri was replaced by Omri, the most wicked king yet (16:25-26). The stage is now set for Ahab, the reigning king during the prophetic ministry of Elijah.

The Word of the LORD

Like a diamond against a backdrop of black velvet, the wickedness of Elijah's day highlights the workings of God through Elijah and causes the full beauty of what God was doing to be seen. Today we will see that the *"word of the Lord"* (1 Kings 17:1 ff.) coming to Elijah was Jehovah's gracious intervention to turn Israel away from their wickedness and back to following God. It was God who took the initiative. Even the drought Elijah prophesied, although an indication of judgment, is evidence of God's grace. He is unwilling to leave us when we stray from Him. He always calls us back. Since the Northern Kingdom (the northern ten tribes of Israel) split from Judah and the kingly line of David, they had given themselves to idols. King after king followed the wicked example of Jeroboam in worshiping the Canaanite gods. Judah meanwhile was enjoying revival under Asa and Hezekiah. But God had not forgotten His people in the Northern Kingdom. He faithfully sent truth to them through the prophet Elijah.

📖 To appreciate Elijah, we must understand the context by which his life is framed. Read 1 Kings 16:29-34 and write what you learn about the reign of king Ahab.

SERVANT APPROACH LEADERSHIP TRAINING: Building Biblical Philosophy   (revised 2/20/223)

ELIJAH (CONTINUED)

Ahab became king of Israel (the northern ten tribes) during the time that Asa was king of Judah (the southern two tribes). Ahab did more evil before the Lord than did all the kings before him. The sins of Jeroboam (see 14:8-9) were trivial compared to Ahab's. He took a pagan wife, and she led him into Baal worship. He also erected the "Asherah" (wooden idols of a female deity).

As if all of Ahab's wickedness weren't enough, verse 34 indicates that during his reign, he allowed Jericho to be rebuilt despite the prohibition of God through Joshua when Israel first came to the promised land. At the culmination of the fall of Jericho, God led Joshua to require the victorious Israelites to take an oath that the man who dared to rebuild Jericho would be cursed of the Lord. This prophecy also claimed that the one who would lay the foundation for the reconstruction of Jericho would do so with the loss of his first-born and would set up the gates with the loss of his youngest son (see Joshua 6:26). It was a pagan custom to dedicate the gates and walls of a new city by burying children inside the foundations. As we see here, all that God promised came to pass. These events set the stage for the new prophet, Elijah.

📖 What, according to 1 Kings 17:1, is Elijah's prophecy regarding Israel?

Elijah began by saying, *"As the Lord, the God of Israel lives..."* Everything that was going to happen was to give evidence to prodigal Israel, that the God of their fathers still lives. Elijah prophesied that there would be *"neither rain nor dew"* in the land for a long, long time except by his word. James 5:17 reminds us that this drought lasted for three years and six months.

📖 Read through 1 Kings 17 and mark every reference to *"the word of the Lord"* and what you learn about it.

The phrase appears five times in this chapter (vs. 2, 5, 8, 16, and 24). In verse 2 we see it as direct communication to Elijah from God. In verse 5 we see that Elijah obeyed the word of the Lord. In verse 8 we see it again as direct communication from the Lord. In verse 16 we see that it was fulfilled, and that it was spoken through Elijah. In verse 24 we see the widow of Zarephath affirming that the word of the Lord was in Elijah's mouth and that the word was true. In addition to these direct references, it is implied in verse 8 that the word of the Lord had already come to the widow of Zarephath (*"... I have commanded a widow there..."*) about providing for him. Though verse 14 doesn't use the phrase, it is obvious God is speaking a word through Elijah (*"...thus says the Lord"*). Verse 15 speaks of *"the word of Elijah"* which he told us in verse 14 was *"thus says the Lord."*

Based on what you observed about the *"word of the Lord,"* what would you conclude about the origin of the prophecy concerning the drought?

SERVANT APPROACH LEADERSHIP TRAINING: Building Biblical Philosophy

ELIJAH (CONTINUED)

It would seem apparent that Elijah was a prophet accustomed to hearing from God and that he simply reported what God had told him. The idea of the drought originated with God, not Elijah.

What do you think God taught Elijah through the situations with the ravens and the widow?

In both situations God's supernatural provision met Elijah's needs. As Elijah was obedient, he enjoyed God's provision, first through the ravens and then through the widow's oil and flour. Following God had placed Elijah in great need, but God was faithful to meet those needs. Even if he didn't follow God, Elijah still would have had the same needs (because of the drought), but if he had not followed God, he would not have experienced God's provision. It is worth noting that the brook Cherith dried up before the word of the Lord came to Elijah about the widow of Zarephath. In the situation with the widow's son, we see Elijah's faith being built by answered prayer.

A "God-initiated" Ministry

True ministry is initiated by God, which means that it is **received**, not achieved. In Acts 20:24 Paul says, *"But I do not consider my life of any account as dear to myself, in order that I may finish my course, and the ministry which I received from the Lord Jesus, to testify solemnly of the gospel of the grace of God."* You see, Paul recognized that his ministry was something he received from the Lord, not something he achieved on his own. In fact, the ministry he was trying to achieve went opposite to the one he would receive. We see this same idea reflected in Colossians 4:17 where Archippus is instructed, *"Take heed to the ministry which you have received in the Lord, that you may fulfill it."* A received ministry means that we are doing God's work, not just good works. This truth is clearly seen in 1 Peter 4:10 where we read, *"As each one has received a special gift, employ it in serving one another, as good stewards of the manifold grace of God."* One of the clearest manifestations of a received ministry is our spiritual giftedness. We had no say in the gifts God gave us. We did nothing to earn or achieve them. We received them from the Lord. A God-initiated ministry comes only through following God in a relationship of dependence. It begins with Him and requires that we hear from Him, and to do so, we must walk in fellowship with Him. That is what following God is all about. We see this principle illustrated beautifully in Elijah's challenge to the prophets of Baal.

📖 Read 1 Kings 18. Now, looking at verse 1, why did Elijah go to Ahab?

The obvious truth here is that going to meet with Ahab was not Elijah's idea; it was God's. Elijah was simply obeying the *"word of the Lord."*

SERVANT APPROACH LEADERSHIP TRAINING: Building Biblical Philosophy

ELIJAH (CONTINUED)

📖 Look through chapter 18 again and write down the details of Elijah's proposal to Ahab and Israel.

Elijah challenged Ahab to assemble for a showdown between God and Baal. Elijah called for an assembly of the whole nation along with the 850 false prophets (450 prophets of Baal and 400 prophets of the Asherah [v.19]) and there suggested the idea of a contest to see which god was strongest. He proposed that oxen be sacrificed and placed on the altar, and that each side would be allowed to call on their God to answer with fire.

📖 What is the result of this proposal?

Baal's prophets called out to their god all day with no response, and then it was Elijah's turn. He called the people near and repaired the altar of the Lord. He had water poured on the offering and then prayed a short prayer. Then *"the fire of the Lord"* fell and consumed the sacrifice. In the end the people fell on their faces and declared, *"The Lord, He is God."* After years of decline, the nation of Israel turned back to the Lord.

📖 The next question is a key one when we look at this issue of a "received" ministry. According to verse 36, did the idea for this challenge to the prophets of Baal come from Elijah or from God?

Verse 36 makes it clear that Elijah did all of these things *"... at **Thy** word."* As we have seen repeatedly, Elijah was not thinking up ideas and asking God to bless them. He was walking in a relationship with God, following Him, and simply obeying what the Lord told him to do.

📖 Compare Elijah's prayer of verse 41-46 with verse 1 of chapter 18 and also James 5:16-18 and write your observations.

We see in James 5 that Elijah's prayer was identified as *"effective prayer."* It is noteworthy that he was not asking God to perform some uncertain task, but rather as 1 Kings 18:1 reveals, he was simply asking God to do what He had already intended to do. Effective prayer is not us coming up with an idea and asking God to fulfill it, but us trusting God to do what He has said He will do. This underscores what Jesus says in John 15:7-8 that before you can *"ask whatever you wish, and it shall be done for you,"* you must abide in Him and allow His words (Scripture) to abide in you.

SERVANT APPROACH LEADERSHIP TRAINING: Building Biblical Philosophy   (revised 2/20/223)

Elijah (continued)

NOTE TAKING OUTLINE #1:

I. Walking with God means Doing <u>His</u> Work, not <u>Ours</u>. (1 Kings 17-18)

    A. True Ministry is _____, not _____

Acts 20:24 – "…*that I may finish my course and the ministry I _____ from the Lord Jesus…*"

Colossians 4:17 – "*And say to Archippus, 'Take heed to the ministry you have _____ in the Lord, that you may fulfill it.'*"

1 Peter 4:10 – "*As each one has _____ a special gift, employ it in serving one another…*"

    B. Elijah's ministry was Received, not Achieved – The theme of his life was:
        "the _____ of the Lord" (1 Kings 17:2, 5, 8, 14, 15, 16, 24)

    C. Mt. Carmel - God's showdown (1 Kings 18)

        450 Baal Prophets & 400 Asherah Prophets

        1 Prophet of Jehovah: Elijah

Key Verse: 18:36: "*…that I have done all these things _____ _____.*"
Main Point:

God has to _____ before we have anything to _____ or _____.

Application:

When we cease to do _____ work, the work gets _____ because we do what we have no grace for.

SERVANT APPROACH LEADERSHIP TRAINING: Building Biblical Philosophy

ELIJAH (CONTINUED)

Bible Study Segment #2:
"Highs" and "Lows" of Following God

When we follow God into a received ministry, whatever that ministry may be, one of the things we must realize is that just because it is God-initiated, that doesn't mean it will always be easy. In a God-initiated ministry there will be high places where we see God move and work in miraculous ways. But there will also be low places. And quite often the low places follow on the heels of the high places. Elijah's encounter with the prophets of Baal on Mount Carmel was a high place, but as we will see today, he did not stay there.

 Read 1 Kings 19:1-8, and looking specifically at verses 1-2, write down a summary of the circumstances which immediately follow the "high place" events of Mount Carmel.

Elijah was allowed no time to "rest on his laurels." When Jezebel heard the report of what Elijah did on Mount Carmel and of the execution of all the prophets, she vowed her own death if she had not killed Elijah within twenty-four hours.

 What, according to verses 3-4, was Elijah's response to Jezebel's threat?

 We know Elijah was a man of faith and a model of effective prayer. What exactly is the request of verse 4, and does God answer it or honor it?

Clearly Elijah's response was not one of faith. He became afraid and fled for his life. He then wandered a day's journey into the wilderness to hide himself, and then sat down dejectedly under a juniper tree. Elijah says in verse four, *"It is enough,"* basically meaning, "I give up." Then in that same verse Elijah asks the Lord to take his life. It is significant that there is no "word of the Lord" in response to Elijah's request. Obviously, God did not respect his request, for He did not take Elijah's life.

SERVANT APPROACH LEADERSHIP TRAINING: Building Biblical Philosophy   (revised 2/20/223)

ELIJAH (CONTINUED)

Think of all Elijah had seen the Lord do. He had seen the Lord sustain him miraculously through a three-and-a-half-year drought. He had watched God humble the nation of Israel and humiliate the pagan prophets by sending fire from heaven. Elijah had experienced a direct and immediate answer to his prayers in the form of a heavy shower bringing the drought to an end. He had even witnessed the Lord supernaturally enable him to outrun Ahab's chariot the seventeen miles from Carmel to Jezreel. Yet now we see him running for his life at the threat of one angry woman. We watch him wandering in the wilderness in a sea of depression and giving up under a tree, lamenting his own existence. What a difference a day makes! The profound truth revealed here is that we cannot live today's trials on yesterday's faith. This story also reveals the likelihood that our spiritual highs will be followed by spiritual lows. I believe there are spiritual, emotional, and physical reasons why this is so. In a spiritual "high place" there is usually a sense of euphoria that drains one emotionally and physically as well. This reality is accompanied by the fact that spiritual highs can move our focus onto the miracles and workings of God themselves instead of on the God who gave them. This leaves us spiritually vulnerable.

📖 Look at verses 5-8 and identify all that God did to restore Elijah.

First, He allowed him to rest. Then He provided Elijah with a hot meal and allowed him to rest again. This was followed by another meal and the admonition that the journey ahead was too great. Even though the text does not say that God told Elijah to go to Horeb, that is the implication, for we know Elijah had no previous plans to go anywhere, and the angel spoke of his impending journey. Horeb is another name for Mount Sinai, the mountain of God, and is not a forty-day journey from Beersheba, so apparently Elijah had to travel in a covert, roundabout manner.

What conclusions would you draw from Elijah's experience about managing your own travels from spiritual highs to spiritual lows?

One obvious principle here is that sometimes the most spiritual thing you can do is to have a good meal and get a good night's sleep. We cannot spiritualize physical needs. A second principle is that we shouldn't rely too heavily on our judgment when we are in a low place. Elijah thought that the best escape would come through his death, but God knew better. A third principle is that once we have rested, we need to meet with God, for this was the purpose of Horeb (Sinai), the place where Moses met with God.

ELIJAH (CONTINUED)

NOTE TAKING OUTLINE #2:
I. Walking with God means Doing His Work, not Ours. (1 Kings 17-18)

II. Walking with God means _____ on His _____, not ours. (1 Kings 19:1-8)

    A. Often in life, the _____ follow the _____, and the _____ the high, the _____ the low. Immediately after Mt. Carmel, Jezebel vows Elijah's death.

    B. What Elijah has _____:

        He saw God…
- sustain him miraculously (ravens, widow's oil) through 3 ½ year drought
- humble Israel, humiliate pagans, bring fire from heaven
- bring revival to entire nation
- answer his prayers for rain
- give him supernatural ability to outrun Ahab's chariot 17 miles from Carmel to Jezreel

        THEN, Jezebel vows his death (19:1-2)

    C. What Elijah _____…

- Elijah was afraid and _____ for his life (19:3-4)
- Ran to _____
- Then a day's journey into the _____
- Sits down under a juniper tree
- _____ up
- Asks God to _____ him

Main Point:

We cannot face today's _____ with yesterday's _____ or experiences.

How does God deal with Elijah?
    1. A few good nights' _____ & some hot _____.

    2. Then He calls him to Horeb – to _____ with _____.

Application:

When we cease to _____ on His life, ministry becomes _____.

ELIJAH (CONTINUED)

Bible Study Segment #3:
"I Alone Am Left..."

What an adventure this has been! After three-and-half years of drought where Elijah hid from Ahab and was miraculously provided for, then came the great showdown on Mount Carmel. Elijah saw God do the things that only God can do. Fire fell from heaven and consumed the sacrifice. Revival broke out among the people. In answer to a brief prayer, the drought finally came to an end. But then events seemingly took a sour turn for Elijah. Jezebel vowed his death. Elijah was devastated, despondent, and an attitude of hopelessness pervaded him. Then God sent help to him and fed him, but his depression did not immediately subside. He spent the next forty days slinking around from Beersheeba to Horeb. Elijah had recovered somewhat from his spiritual valley, yet he still needed to meet with God and begin to see things from His perspective.

📖 Look at 1 Kings 19:9-10 and identify Elijah's perspective on the situation and what you think is wrong with it.

Elijah began by contrasting his own zeal for God with that of the nation of Israel, who had abandoned the Lord. He reminded God that all the other prophets had been killed, and then he says in verse 10, *"I alone am left; and they seek my life..."* It almost seems that Elijah was saying, God, I'm all you have left and they're about to kill me too!" Elijah's focus is on himself instead of the Lord, and the implication is that God needed Elijah's help.

📖 What does God do in verses 11 and 12 to alter Elijah's perspective, and according to verse 14, did it work?

God manifested Himself to Elijah and demonstrated His power. It would seem that the manifestations of the *"great and strong wind,"* the earthquake, the fire, and the gentle breeze served to give Elijah a higher view of God, yet as we see in verse 14, his perspective had not changed any from verse 10.

📖 Looking at verses 15-18, identify what God did next and how that might relate to Elijah's view that he was the only one left who followed God.

God gave Elijah the assignment of anointing Hazael, Jehu, and Elisha, and indicated that in addition to them, He had seven thousand who had not bowed to Baal. What a far cry from Elijah's prideful view that he was all that God had left. Rather than bluntly saying, "Elijah, you are wrong," God tactfully brought to the forefront all the others in Israel (Northern Kingdom) who stood for God.

SERVANT APPROACH LEADERSHIP TRAINING: Building Biblical Philosophy (revised 2/20/223)

ELIJAH (CONTINUED)

As you will see in the rest of Elijah's life and ministry, Elisha was a gift from God to him—a friend, a disciple, and the one who would continue his ministry when Elijah was gone. Sometimes when we follow God in the midst of those who are antagonistic toward the gospel, we become ensnared in the trap of pride, believing that God needs us because we follow when others don't. But God is totally self-sufficient. Like a loving father, He allows us to join Him in His work, but He **does not need** our help. As Mordecai told Queen Esther when she struggled with interceding with the king for Israel, *"… if you remain silent at this time, relief and deliverance will arise for the Jews from another place and you and your father's house will perish."* In other words, "Don't think you are indispensable, for if you don't help us, God will provide relief from somewhere else, but you and your family won't get to have a part in it." We must always guard against the prideful notion that just because we follow God, He needs our help.

NOTE TAKING OUTLINE #3:

I. Walking with God means Doing His Work, not Ours. (1 Kings 17-18)

II. Walking with God means drawing on His life, not ours. (1 Kings 19:1-8)

III. Walking with God means _____ on _____, not ourselves. (1 Kings 19:9-18)
    A. Elijah _____ with God at Horeb

        God says… *"What are you doing here, Elijah?"*
        Elijah's says…
            "_____ *have been zealous…"*
            "_____ *alone am left…"*

        Then God _____ His _____ (vs. 11-13)

        God says… *"What are you doing here, Elijah?"*
        Elijah's says…
            "_____ *have been zealous…"*
            "_____ *alone am left…"*

Elijah is saying, *"God, You'd better do something because ____ _____ _____ _____ _____ and they're trying to kill me."*

    B. Elijah's wrong _____ is a _____ Problem
        Doesn't understand that:

           God _____ Elijah = God _____ Elijah
           Not "_____ 1" but 1+3+_____

Main Point:

We only see things in their proper perspective when our _____ are on _____.

Application:
When we cease to _____ on Him, ministry becomes _____.

SERVANT APPROACH LEADERSHIP TRAINING: Building Biblical Philosophy

ELIJAH (CONTINUED)

Bible Study Segment #4: Application Homework

This last portion is for you to do as homework, looking to how you need to apply what you have learned about received ministry.

For Me To Follow God

It has been said that "You are the only Bible some people will ever read." That statement presents to us an awesome responsibility. Yet it should be considered an awesome privilege. We must all be quick to recognize that our walk with God has an effect on those around us. More is at stake in our relationship with God than just our own walk, for if we live yielded to Him, then He can minister to others through us. James says an interesting thing about Elijah. In James 5:17 he says, *"Elijah was a man **with a nature like ours**..."* (emphasis mine). When we look at Elijah and what God did through him, we are tempted to place him into a separate category of super saints. But he was a man **like us**! As such, he is an example of how God wants to use us as agents of revival in our day. However, for that to happen, our study of Elijah must go beyond a mere collection of information. We must take the truths of God's word and put them into application.

One of the lessons we learn from Elijah is that following God means doing **His** work, not our own work. Elijah's ministry was **received**, not achieved. He didn't try to make a ministry happen on his own. He met with God and then responded to His leading. An achieved ministry, one that is initiated by man instead of by God, is of no consequence in eternity—and is also much more difficult to maintain. When we cease to do His work, the work gets burdensome because we are trying to perform tasks without the grace that only God can give.

Can you see any examples in your own life or those around you of ministry that is **achieved** (man-initiated) instead of **received** (initiated by God)?

To have a received ministry, we must hear from God before we act. The oft-repeated refrain of Elijah's life was *"...the word of the Lord came to him."* What this makes clear is that the Word must come before the work. We need a regular diet of God's Word if we want to see Him minister through us to others.

Looking at the list below, check every area where you currently receive biblical input.

- ❏ Sermons at church
- ❏ Religious TV
- ❏ Conferences
- ❏ Bible Study group
- ❏ Personal Bible reading
- ❏ Podcasts
- ❏ Books
- ❏ Magazines
- ❏ Study workbooks such as this one
- ❏ Other _____
- ❏ Christian radio
- ❏ Devotionals
- ❏ Counselor

Now, take a moment to look back through each of the places you marked and ask yourself, "Does that source take me to what the Word of God has to say, or does it merely take me to what man has to say about God?"

ELIJAH (CONTINUED)

Are there any changes toward which the Lord is prompting you in this area?

Another key principle we see in the life of Elijah is that following God means drawing on **His** life, not ours. When Elijah wandered out into the wilderness to die, it was clear that he was no longer drawing on the resources of God's strength but was walking in his own strength. When we cease to draw on the life of God, ministry becomes a fearful thing. We find Elijah running for his life from Jezebel, even though a few hours before, he single-handedly faced down the prophets of Baal. There is an important lesson here: **We cannot face today's trials with yesterday's faith or experiences.**

When Elijah wanted to die, God had two solutions to his despondency—rest and revelation. First, Elijah needed physical rejuvenation. We cannot spiritualize physical needs. Sometimes the most spiritual thing we can do is to eat a good meal and to get a good night's rest.

If you are depressed or despondent, are you taking care of your physical body?

What do you need to do differently?

While we cannot overlook the physical, we cannot look only there either. Once the physical was taken care of, Elijah still had a need. So God called him to Horeb (Sinai), the mountain of God. Are you facing fears and obstacles? Perhaps you need to get alone with God. Make time to do this.

To draw on the life of God, we must be surrendered to Him. He must be in control of our hearts. When He is in control, we never lack power for the tasks He gives us. Is every area of your heart yielded to Him? If not, take time to do that now.

A third principle we see in Elijah is that following God means focusing on **Him**, not ourselves. When Elijah came to Horeb to meet with God, his prayer was filled with self-pity and self-focus. He said, *"I have been zealous..."* and *"I alone am left ..."* Even after God revealed Himself to Elijah in a majestic way, his prayer was repeated unchanged. In essence, he said, "God, You'd better do something because I'm all You have left and they're trying to kill me."

Elijah's problem really was a math problem. He had not learned the truth of the equation listed below:

$$\text{God} + \text{Elijah} = \text{God} - \text{Elijah}$$

God chooses to use us, but He does not need us. He is complete—He has no needs. The Scriptures teach us that if we do not preach the gospel, the rocks and trees will cry out (see Luke 19:40). Yet as a loving Father, though He does not require our help, He desires our help. He invites us to join Him in His work. He does not want us working on our own, independent of Him, and He will not bless such labor.

Take a moment to reflect honestly on your service to the Lord. Have you seen any evidences in your heart of thinking God needed your help and was blessed to have you on His team? If so, confess that sin of pride to Him.

ELIJAH (CONTINUED)

Not only did Elijah so focus on himself as to think that God could not do without him, but he also had so focused on himself as to think that he was all God had. Yet immediately God sent him to anoint three servants and make him aware of the 7,000 others of whom Elijah didn't even know.

Have you ever prayed, "I alone am left"?

Ask God to show you the other faithful servants around you that you haven't seen before. If we lose our focus on Him, ministry (and life) becomes a lonely place. If there are evidences of Elijah at Horeb in your heart, you need to stop focusing on yourself and start focusing on Him.

Let's spend some time in prayer to the Lord right now.

Lord, thank You for this very human example of Elijah. I thank You for the ministry I have received from You. Help me to be faithful to the tasks You have given me. Guard me from trying to achieve something else. Make me quick to listen for You and patient to wait for "the Word of the Lord" to come, so that I am doing YOUR work and not just good works. I long to draw on Your life, to walk in Your strength and not my own. Show me quickly when I am not doing that. Give me faith for today and help me to focus on You and not me. I confess that You don't require my help, and I praise You that You still desire it. Thank You for inviting me into Your work. Help me to be faithful. Amen.

SESSION 1: HOMEWORK SUMMARY

Due Date: _____

Review of homework assignments:

Building a Biblical Philosophy of Ministry

© Copyright 2005 Eddie Rasnake
You may reproduce this chapter at no charge as long as proper credit is given and no changes are made to the document

What is a "Biblical Philosophy" of ministry?

I realize that for many, the term "Biblical Philosophy" is an unfamiliar term. For some, it sounds like two components that don't fit with each other. Perhaps there is an association in our minds between the term "philosophy" and the class we took in college by the same name. I once heard a philosopher compared to "a blind person in a dark room looking for a black cat that isn't there." I must confess that this description fit my college class well. Why don't we like the term "philosophy?" There is a Biblical admonition to be concerned with it.

📖 Read Colossians 2:8.

According to this verse, what should not shape our thinking?

To what is this particular kind of philosophy contrasted?

Colossians 2:8 advises, "*See to it that no one takes you captive through philosophy and empty deception, according to the traditions of men, according to the elementary principles of the world, rather than according to Christ.*" We must lay our anchor to absolute truth, or we will drift with every wind and wave of the latest ideas and fads. Notice however that Colossians 2:8 does not say all philosophy is wrong. According to this verse, wrong philosophies are those whose origin is in the traditions of men rather than the Word of God. The term "philosophy" is Greek in origin. It is made up of two Greek roots: *philos* (meaning "friend") and *sophia* (meaning "wisdom"). The two words together literally mean "to be a friend of wisdom." Now that doesn't sound so bad, does it? Philosophy can be good if it is a love of true wisdom. Of course, the ultimate source of that kind of wisdom is Christ and His Word. In Colossians 2:8 Paul contrasts the philosophies of men (which are to be avoided) with right philosophies – those which are "*...according to Christ.*" When we study and understand the teachings of Scripture, bringing all the truths that God's Word has to say on a matter into balance with each other, the product is a "Biblical Philosophy." What I mean by the term is the recognition of the whole of Biblical values in a particular area so we can then apply those values as we seek to live out God's will in that specific arena. For example, a Biblical philosophy of missions would first identify a balanced view of what the Scriptures teach about missions, and then would use that view to define in practical terms the right and wrong approaches to missions.

Defining a Biblical Philosophy

If Biblical philosophy is to be our goal, how do we arrive at that? Consider the example I mentioned of missions. Few would argue whether or not missions is Biblical, yet the way missions is approached and practiced can and sometimes does run contrary to Scripture. This scenario isn't usually a result of people abandoning the Bible. Sometimes the problem lies in holding to an imbalanced view of what the Bible

BUILDING A BIBLICAL PHILOSOPHY OF MINISTRY (CONT.)

teaches. In other words, the Scriptures have been **inadequately examined**. We operate without having all the information and instruction God has given, and as a result, what we do is not fully what He desires. Another reason for wrong practice is that God's instructions have been **inaccurately interpreted**. If we misunderstand what God has said, with a good heart we will misapply that information. In addition, sometimes wrong practice results from **insufficiently distinguishing** what is explicitly Biblical from those portions of our values and practice which have their origin in our culture and tradition. Because the whole counsel of Scripture has not first been completely examined, man's traditions and ideas and the values of our culture end up being given equal weight with Scripture. A fourth cause of origin for wrong practice is that the truths of God have been **incompletely applied**. Often our errors are not sins of commission (doing what God has instructed us not to do), but rather are sins of omission (not doing all that God has told us to do).

Consider how the mistakes of inadequate examination, inaccurate interpretation, insufficient distinction, and incomplete application of Scripture can result in a flawed obedience. People are lost without God and in need of salvation, but that truth alone is not enough. Armed with that premise alone, the Crusades sought to convert the Middle East by military force. The imbalance of holding to one truth only came at the expense of other Biblical values like love and the importance of heart change instead of lip service to Christianity. In like manner, the missionary conquest of Africa a century and a half ago carried the gospel message, but in their culturally biased quest to make Christians out of those "African heathens," many missionaries promoted Western or European dress and culture as being of equal importance to Biblical morality and a repentant heart toward God. Their message was such a mixture of the Biblical and the cultural that in effect, one came away with a sense that they had to convert to being British or American to convert to Christianity. **While the result was wrong behavior, it was often performed with a right heart.** The problems here occurred because practical applications were arrived at without first allowing the demands of ALL that Scripture says about missions to bring each specific Biblical value to a place of balance with the rest. We must balance the tensions of all Biblical mission values before designing our approach to missions. We will consider what that balance of Biblical values might look like a little later in the process, when we look at our Philosophy of Missions.

How do we balance the tension of Biblical values? We must collect all the relevant truths presented in Scripture and rightly interpret them. Then we must weave them together in a balance of their demands and definitions rather than holding one to excess. The better we identify the Biblical values, the easier it becomes to arrive at a right practice. Scripture will show us what to do and how to do it. At the same time, it will be eliminating that which is out of line with God's will and way. Though taking the time to define the Biblical values delays our identifying a practice and plan of attack, it insures we end up doing the right things in the way God wants them done. As I seek to balance the tension of Biblical values, I look not only for those specific references to the subject at hand, but also to the principles of other passages, and those theological boundaries of God's attributes and sound doctrine that come to bear on the matter. The product of defining a practice out of balanced Biblical values is what I am calling a "Biblical philosophy."

The impact of Biblical Philosophy on decisions and direction

Every church or ministry makes decisions regularly and this can require a significant investment of time. Unfortunately, in most churches, making decisions takes far more time and effort because the approach is fundamentally flawed. They have not first defined their philosophy Biblically in the particular area of the needed decision. For example, if the mission philosophy of a church hasn't been fully discussed and defined, making a decision on supporting or sending individual missionaries becomes a subjective

BUILDING A BIBLICAL PHILOSOPHY OF MINISTRY (CONT.)

process dominated by personal biases. Some decisions in that process get repeated with each new candidate when they could have been answered once and for all by a defined Biblical philosophy. In fact, some candidates would be eliminated altogether, saving them and the decision-making body a lot of time. The same holds true in budgeting. How can a church evaluate its budget without a defined philosophy that reflects Biblical financial priorities? It cannot do so in any objective way. Instead, it will tend to evaluate based on past budgets, and end up repeating past mistakes and imbalances.

Since every decision-making body – whether a finance committee, board of directors, deacon body, council of elders, missions committee or something else – has a finite amount of time. Without good definition of a Biblical philosophy in their task, negative results inevitably creep in. First, there is a tendency to make incomplete decisions. When the time crunch hits, committees cannot devote much time to debating philosophy. Sooner or later they will decide that enough (or too much) time has been devoted to that topic while other decisions are also pressing. Sometimes they then succumb to the temptation of making a "lowest common denominator" decision that all can agree upon instead of coming to a thoroughly Biblical resolution. Another common mistake is to table the issue without arriving at a Biblical resolution. The result is a decision by default. By deciding not to decide, for all practical purposes they decide to do nothing, even when action may be Biblically required of them.

Though many decision-making bodies feel they do not have enough time to fully define philosophy (Biblical values), they are actually wasting time by not doing so. The next time the issue arises, they will have the same debates once again. In addition, in the absence of a clearly defined Biblical philosophy we tend to make mistakes even when correcting mistakes. Without the core values and practices that a Biblical philosophy brings to our evaluation, it is easy to react to a problem with an equally problematic solution. We make decisions that we later regret. By not taking time to do it right, we must make time to do it over. When a church or ministry defines who they are, they also define who they are not. The result is that every decision that follows becomes easier to make.

The impact of Biblical philosophy on evaluating personal actions

A clear definition of Biblical philosophy helps us make decisions, but it also guards us from mixing our opinions with God's Word. Not only does this serve a leadership team well, but it aids the individual as well. Consider the issue of a Christian worker drinking wine. Is this permissible or prohibited? Most who read this are quickly drawing a mental verdict of right and wrong in the equation. Let me urge you to be careful, for in so doing, most will tend to go further in one direction than Scripture does while not going far enough in others. The Bible does identify drunkenness as sin. It also marks it as wrong to cause your brother to stumble. But don't stop there. As a pastor, I have decided to avoid even moderate use of alcohol, but Biblical integrity demands I admit that it is drunkenness – not drinking – that the Bible forbids. Though cultural concerns motivate me to add a measure of personal deference to the prohibitions of Scripture, I cannot impose that extra-Biblical boundary as a rule for anyone but myself.
When we want to prove grey areas are wrong, we tend to rely on the "causing someone to stumble" argument. It would serve us well to remember that though black and white are absolute are at ends of the spectrum, gray exists in shades. I have noticed with such colors that the less light there is, the darker the shade appears. What seems dark gray in the dim light of dawn may be revealed as a different shade in the extra light that comes as the sun rises. I think this holds true with legalism. It is the light of further study which drives it away.

Building a Biblical Philosophy of Ministry (cont.)

📖 Look at Romans 14.

What does Paul tell us we should do (see 14:5, 14, 22)?

What does Paul tell us we should not do (see 14:1, 3, 4, 10, 13, 16, 20, 21)?

Romans 14 challenges each of us to "*be fully convinced in his own mind*" (Romans 14:5 emphasis mine, see also 14:14 and 22). Though Paul urges us to aggressively work toward developing our own convictions, his repeated call is for us to "*accept*" others when we disagree. Even after our convictions are solid, we need to allow time for God's maturing work to bring others to a balanced view of Scripture (see Romans 14:1 and 15:7). Our responsibility is to pursue that balance for ourselves, not others. This familiar passage which admonishes us to avoid causing others to stumble, also dictates that our personal convictions not be used to judge the convictions of others. That prohibition doesn't get as much pulpit-play. Consider this though – the principle of "*stumbling blocks*" is warned against four times in this chapter (twice in Romans 14:13, once each in 14:20 and 14:21), while "*judging*" is identified as wrong and negatively represented nine times (Romans 14:1, twice in 14:3, 14:4, three times in 14:10, 14:13, and 14:16). We must take care not to add cultural or personal preference to the directives of Scripture. It was also in the context of judging that Paul admonished the Corinthians of the need to "*learn not to exceed what is written, so that no one of you will become arrogant in behalf of one against the other*" (1 Corinthians 4:6). In violating this important principle, the Pharisees converted the Ten Commandments into 613 rules (248 commands and 365 prohibitions), which later were bolstered into 1521 emendations (*The Jesus I Never Knew*, Philip Yancey, Zondervan Publishing House, p.132). Each extension was probably an attempt to address a perceived problem and to try to ensure that no one got out of line.

Developing Biblical Convictions

I believe to arrive at Biblical convictions is always a process, and the more time given to it, the more trustworthy the outcome. We probably don't even recognize this in our personal Christian values, but quite often what we consider to be Biblical convictions are really just opinions. What is the difference? Paul identified that we should make it our goal to be "*fully convinced.*" The Greek word in Romans 14:5 that Paul's phrase is translated from (*plerophoreo*—Strong's #4135) implies a certainty and completion to the study process. Paul had arrived at such a place regarding "*unclean*" foods and beverages (see Romans 14:14). His thinking had matured to the point of confidently drawing a conclusion before the Lord on the matter. He was not convinced because of personal preference on the matter or cultural biases. Paul was raised as a Jew. Having also been a Pharisee, the starting point of his opinion on the matter would have been influenced from his strict observation of the dietary laws. Those ran the opposite direction. He was "*convinced in the Lord Jesus.*" He based his conclusion only on Christ and His Word. That well illustrates what a conviction is. Until we have thoroughly studied all that Scripture has to say on a matter, what we believe is still opinion, and is probably influenced by culture and preference. Much damage is done to the cause of Christ by the divisiveness of letting inadequately studied opinions masquerade as convictions.

The Jerusalem council in Acts 15 was a pivotal historical event in the life of the early church. At stake was whether a Gentile needed to become a Jew to be a Christian. The question forced the early church to evaluate their view of salvation and sort out which portions were Scriptural mandates with the authority of God, and which were merely cultural biases. They did not start out in agreement. Opinions were passionately debated (see Acts 15:7). The unity of early believers was on the verge of fracture. Many

BUILDING A BIBLICAL PHILOSOPHY OF MINISTRY (CONT.)

churches have split and denominations have even been formed over far less significant issues. In the end, the apostles and elders concluded that circumcision should be viewed as part of Jewish culture, heritage and tradition, but not part of Christian salvation. Perhaps the most powerful reflection of God speaking through the process is the simple phrase in James' letter, "...*having become of one mind*" (Acts 15:25). This unity gives divine evidence that they were able to bring the matter to conclusion. As we read the chapter though, it is obvious that conclusion was not drawn until all that God had revealed was thoroughly considered. Once there was a unified finality, they wrote their conclusions down and passed them out to the churches to be put into practice.

A Practical Process

How do we arrive at a trustworthy Biblical philosophy? I would like to offer some suggestions, but I caution you from considering these (or the product they produce) as being exhaustive. I place the greatest confidence in convictions shaped over time and much study, as well as the refining examination of others. There is an unshakable confidence in such matters because the authority behind it is God and His word rather than limited human reasoning. We see this kind of confidence in Martin Luther at the Diet of Worms. His convictions came from a thorough study of Scripture and were strong enough to stand against all the might of Rome. Mere opinions give no such confidence. Paul calls each of us to invest the time and energy it takes to be "*fully convinced*" by the Word of God. Let me suggest some practical steps to follow.

Step 1: Study thoroughly. We must study everything Scripture explicitly teaches on the specific matter. Consider the book of the Revelation. Perhaps no portion of Scripture foments so much disagreement and fanciful ideas. G. K. Chesterton wrote, "...though St. John the Evangelist saw many strange monsters in his vision, he saw no creature so wild as one of his own commentators" (*Orthodoxy*, G. K. Chesterton, New York: Dodd, Mead & co., p.9). I am convinced that part of the reason for this is that the eschatology (doctrine of the end times) of many is based solely on Revelation. The problem is, although there are 480 verses in Revelation, there are over 500 references to the Old Testament. One cannot hope to accurately interpret Revelation without also considering the Old Testament prophecies and weaving Revelation into all that Scripture reveals of the end times. Much disagreement exists because most have not taken anywhere near enough time to draw legitimate conclusions. Instead, they have borrowed convictions (or opinions) from those they respect, insufficiently supported them with limited study, and then dared to call them convictions. Without considering the whole counsel of God, there can be no finality to our conclusions. The Bible sheds a lot of light on my opinions, and in the process shows many of them to be either wrong or incomplete. The starting point of a Biblical philosophy on a matter is to study in context every explicit reference the Bible contains on that subject.

Step 2: Interpret accurately. Once we have studied thoroughly, we must make sure we interpret accurately. For an interpretation to be trustworthy, our conclusion of what the passage means must be consistent with the immediate context, with the complete Word of God, with the culture of the time understood, with consideration of the common understanding, and with a view to theological consistency. No matter how sincere we are in wanting to apply God's Word, we are still prone to err if that application is based on wrong interpretation. This requires we consider not only those passages directly addressing our subject, but also those whose principles address the matter indirectly.

Step 3: Open your conclusions to the scrutiny of others. It was only with the help of others that some of those Jews in the Jerusalem council were able to refine their opinions and beliefs to the point of them becoming convictions. I always want to hear what someone who disagrees has to say. By listening to

BUILDING A BIBLICAL PHILOSOPHY OF MINISTRY (CONT.)

them with intellectual honesty, being persuadable to the Word of God, I have almost always been practically benefited. Sometimes their Biblical counterpoints have changed my conclusion. Other times, the weakness of their arguments have galvanized my confidence in a Scriptural conclusion. Often, they have revealed incompleteness in my study and flaws in my interpretation. I do not need to fear the Word of God showing me to be wrong. I am all the better for it.

Step 4: Refine your conclusions into convictions. The ancient Greeks viewed learning as a three-stage process. This "classical" education consisted of grammar, logic, and rhetoric. In Grammar one sought to understand all of the information – the facts. Logic was the process of weaving those facts together into a harmonious (non-contradictory) way of thinking. They did not consider the matter fully understood however, without rhetoric. Rhetoric was the ability to take the facts, having woven them into a philosophy, and then articulate them clearly to someone else in an understandable manner. They considered rhetoric as attaining the highest level of understanding. I believe that to refine our conclusions into convictions, we must reduce them to their most basic form. We must be able to state them fairly, simply, and convincingly.

Step 5: Translate your convictions into specific actions. Howard Hendricks, the consummate communicator and eminent theologian from Dallas Seminary, said well, "To know and not to do is not to know at all." Once we have convictions, we must apply them to our lives and ministries. We must let them shape and dictate our practice. The more specifically we define ourselves (assuming we have done so Biblically and accurately), the easier decisions on the matter become from that point forward. We know what to do and what to avoid. We know not only the will of God, but also the way in which God desires us to follow His will. **I want to make sure you don't miss this one point. It is not enough to have Biblical values…we must shape them into a practical, culturally relevant system or plan of action. Equally important however, is this—if we develop a practical plan without first defining the Biblical values, we will end up deifying pragmatism. We will define as right any plan that brings results, without respecting that God's will must be done in God's way.**

When we implement these five steps, on the other side of them we find ourselves armed with a Biblical philosophy that serves to define us. One of the great tragedies of the body of Christ in our generation is that so much of what we believe is undefined. As a result, so much of what we practice is indefensible. We must arm ourselves with convictions based solely on the Word of God. It is no use arguing for the inerrancy of the Bible if we are not willing to embrace its authority in our lives. If we do not take the time to define Biblical philosophy, our fate will be that of Israel during that dark period of the Judges: "*In those days there was no king* (i.e. defined authority) *in Israel; everyone did what was right in their own eyes*" (Judges 21:25, parenthesis mine).

BUILDING A BIBLICAL PHILOSOPHY OF MINISTRY (CONT.)

Notes:

Philosophy of Servant Leadership

© Copyright 2005 Eddie Rasnake
You may reproduce this chapter at no charge as long as proper credit is given and no changes are made to the document.

Is there a difference between leadership in the spiritual realm and leadership in general? Though there shouldn't be, there often is. To deny this is to ignore the fallen nature of man and the fallen world in which we live. I once heard leadership defined as "knowing where you are going and being able to persuade others to follow." While that may be a true statement, it says nothing about whether such leadership is good or bad, right or wrong. How does one come to the place of "knowing where they are going?" That, I believe, is what separates leadership in general from spiritual leadership. In the arena of spirituality there is only one true leader – Jesus Christ. He is both the "author and perfecter" of faith (Hebrews 12:2. Interestingly, the Greek word translated "author" (*archegos*) means not only "originator and founder" but also "leader and chief"). Therefore, when we speak of leaders in the human realm, those who lead rightly are always "following leaders." They follow Christ, and also lead others in that same direction. An ungodly leader may have a well-defined plan of where they are heading, but since that plan is not the product of following Christ, it is either of their own, fleshly origination, or it is borrowed from another fallen example they follow.

"Following leaders," if they are following Christ, are able to be the "leading followers." Such a sentence requires reflection to understand the point being made. There is an often-repeated invitation in Scripture to follow God. The birthplace of spiritual battle – the Garden of Eden – was really about whether Eve would follow God or follow Satan; whether Adam would follow God or follow Eve (See Genesis 3:1-6). At the borders of the Promised Land, Israel rejected following the clear leading of God, and instead, enthroned their own reason. The devastating consequence was forty years of wandering. On Mount Carmel, Elijah challenged Israel, "*How long will you hesitate between two opinions? If the Lord is God, follow Him; but if Baal, follow him*" (1 Kings 18:21). Jesus invited those who would be His disciples, "*Follow Me*" (Matthew 4:19, 8:22, 9:9, 16:24, 19:21; Mark 1:17, 2:14, 8:34, 10:21; Luke 5:27, 9:23, 59, 18:22; John 1:43, 10:27, 12:26, 13:36, 21:19, 22). Spiritual leaders – those who lead rightly – are always "following leaders." Therefore, they really should be called the "leading followers." They are those who follow Christ in such a way that they can be followed with confidence by the younger and less mature. Is this truly a Biblical concept?

▢ Read Hebrews 13:7-9 and answer the questions that follow.

What does the Greek word translated "remember" in 13:7 mean?

What does speaking the Word of God have to do with leading?

Why in this context are followers told to "consider the results of a leader's conduct?"

Why are we to imitate a leader's faith instead of the leader?

SERVANT APPROACH LEADERSHIP TRAINING: Building Biblical Philosophy   (revised 2/20/223)

PHILOSOPHY OF SERVANT LEADERSHIP (CONTINUED)

What does Hebrews 13:8 have to do with 13:7?

In Hebrews 13:9, what is being contrasted with the message of grace?

…what does this verse tell us that grace does?

 Read the following passages and summarize their message:

Matthew 20:25-28

Mark 10:35-45

Luke 22:24-2

John 13:1-15

Philippians 2:3-4

PHILOSOPHY OF SERVANT LEADERSHIP (CONTINUED)

Looking for a Leader

When most organizations look for a new leader, be they secular or sacred, they look for the exact opposite of what they really need. Let that sink in for a moment. It is a sober, but fully substantiated reality. It is not an ideological opinion but an empirical fact. Although it is the minority view, it is the only one consistent with the brutal facts. Those facts – an analysis by brilliant minds from the Stanford Business School of 15 years of objective data that compared great companies with good ones that failed to become great – revealed a conclusion no one was looking for. In fact, it was so blatantly obvious as to be seen in spite of the team leader's explicit instructions to "*downplay* the role of the top executives so that we could avoid the simplistic 'credit the leader' or 'blame the leader' thinking common today." When the research team argued for the need to consider the consistently unusual data being generated, team leader Jim Collins kept insisting "ignore the executives!" In his own words, "Finally – as should always be the case – the data won." A main factor present in companies that achieved and sustained a lasting greatness was the absence of a charismatic, dominating personality at the helm. In contrast, the stronger personalities, even if successful in the short run, were more likely to set the company up for freefall or mediocrity than for success when they left. That's the funny thing about truth. It really doesn't matter how you feel about it or what you prefer – it is what it is.

The Misguided Mix-up of Celebrity and Leadership by Jim Collins

Virtually everything our modern culture believes about the type of leadership required to transform our institutions is wrong. It is also dangerous. There is perhaps no more corrosive trend to the health of our organizations than the rise of the celebrity CEO, the rock-star leader whose deepest ambition is first and foremost self-centric. In 1996, my research team and I began to wrestle with a simple question: Can a good company become a great company and, if so, how? If we could find organizations that had made the leap from good to great and isolate the factors that distinguished these examples from carefully selected comparison companies that failed to make the leap (or if they did, failed to sustain it), we would shed light on the key variables that separate great from good. We embarked on a five-year study to answer this one deceptively simple question, examining merely good performers that had somehow transformed themselves to achieve truly great results. (We defined "great results" as cumulative stock returns at least 3.0 times better than the general stock market over fifteen years, a performance superior to most widely admired companies. For perspective, General Electric from 1985 to 2000 beat the market only 2.8 to 1.)

We uncovered a number of key requirements and underlying variables for turning a good company into a great one. But perhaps the most intriguing—and certainly the most surprising—is the type of leadership that turns good into great. Consider Darwin E. Smith. In 1971, this seemingly ordinary man became chief executive of Kimberly-Clark. He inherited a company that for one hundred years had been merely good, never great. A mediocre player in the middling paper industry, Kimberly-Clark returns to investors had fallen 36 percent behind the general stock market over the twenty years prior to Darwin Smith's ascension to CEO. Over the next twenty years, Smith led a stunning turnabout, generating returns to investors that beat the general stock market by over four times, easily outperforming such companies as Hewlett-Packard, General Electric, and Coca-Cola.

Have you ever heard of Darwin Smith? Despite being one of the greatest CEOs of the twentieth century, he remains largely unknown. A shy and reserved man, Smith shunned any attempt to shine the spotlight on him, preferring instead to direct attention to the company and its people. He showed none of the swagger that characterizes many of today's high-profile CEOs, and he never viewed himself as a great

Philosophy of Servant Leadership (continued)

hero. Early in Smith's tenure as CEO, a director pulled Smith aside to remind him that he lacked some of the qualifications for the position (he had been corporate counsel and had never run a major division). Smith, a man who never entirely erased his own self-doubts, later summed up his tenure by saying simply, "I never stopped trying to become qualified for the job."

Yet despite his shy and self-effacing nature, Smith was anything but weak. When it came time to make the big decisions required to make the company great, he made them. Early in his tenure, he unflinchingly decided to sell all the traditional paper mills, which accounted for the majority of Kimberly-Clark's business—sell even the namesake mill in Kimberly, Wisconsin—and throw all the money into the consumer business, investing in brands like Huggies and Kleenex. It was a huge and painful step. Coming home from work during this particularly difficult period, a wearied Smith said to his wife, "It's really tough. But if you have a cancer in your arm, then you've got to have the guts to cut off your arm."

Wall Street derided him, the business media called the move stupid, and the analysts wrote merciless commentary. After all, how on earth could such a mediocre paper company take on the giants of the consumer business? But in the end, Smith's stoic resolve paid off. Kimberly-Clark became the number one paper-based consumer products company in the world, eventually beating Procter & Gamble in six of eight product categories and owning outright its previous main competitor, Scott Paper. I think we can safely say that Darwin Smith did indeed become qualified for the job.

Level 5 leadership: The antithesis of egocentric celebrity
If you want to grasp the essence of the type of leader who turns good into great, just keep in mind Darwin Smith. It turns out that every good-to-great company in our study had a leader from the Darwin Smith school of management at the helm during the pivotal years.

We eventually came to call these remarkable people "Level 5 leaders." The term "Level 5" refers to a five-level hierarchy. Level 1 relates to individual capability, Level 2 to team skills, Level 3 to managerial competence, and Level 4 to leadership as traditionally conceived. Level 5 leaders possess the skills of levels 1 to 4 but also have an "extra dimension": a paradoxical blend of personal humility ("I never stopped trying to become qualified for the job") and professional will ("sell the mills"). They are somewhat self-effacing individuals who deflect adulation, yet who have an almost stoic resolve to do absolutely whatever it takes to make the company great, channeling their ego needs away from themselves and into the larger goal of building a great company. It's not that Level 5 leaders have no ego or self-interest. Indeed, they are incredibly ambitious—*but their ambition is first and foremost for the institution and its greatness, not for themselves.*

David Maxwell, the good-to-great CEO at Fannie Mae in the 1980s and early 1990s, was another such leader. He took over a bureaucratic, quasi-governmental entity losing $1 million every single business day and turned it into one of the smartest, best-run financial institutions in the world, earning $4 million every business day. Fannie Mae cumulative stock returns beat the general stock market by nearly four times under Maxwell, and he set the stage for the next generation to continue the momentum, eventually outperforming the market by over seven times.

When his nearly $20 million retirement package became a point of controversy in Congress (Fannie Mae is subject to congressional oversight due to its government charter), Maxwell became concerned that the controversy might damage the company's future. So he instructed his successor to not pay him the remaining third of his package and to donate it instead to the Fannie Mae foundation for low-income housing.

Philosophy of Servant Leadership (continued)

Like all Level 5 leaders, Maxwell wanted to see the company become even more successful in the next generation than in his own. Preferring to be clock builders rather than time tellers, Level 5 leaders are comfortable with the idea that their companies will tick on without them, reaching even greater heights due to the foundations they laid down. The fact that most people will not know that the roots of that success trace back to them is not an overriding concern. As one Level 5 leader put it, "I want to look out from my porch at one of the great companies of the world and be able to say, 'I used to work there.'"

It is not surprising, then, that some of the greatest CEOs of the last forty years—those few extraordinary executives who led companies from good to great using our tough benchmarks—are relatively unknown. In addition to Darwin Smith and David Maxwell, they include such obscure figures as George Cain, Alan Wurtzel, Colman Mockler, Lyle Everingham, Fred Allen, Joe Cullman, Carl Reichardt and Charles Walgreen III. These and other leaders in our study quietly went about building greatness step by step, without much fanfare or hoopla, while generating results that are extraordinary by any standard. If you had had an opportunity to invest in each of the good-to-great companies at the point of upward inflection created by these leaders and held your investments to 2000, your total returns would have exceeded those of a comparable investment in a mutual fund of the general stock market by well over eight times. Yet despite these remarkable results, almost no one has ever remarked about these leaders. The media paid scant attention, and you'll find very few articles ever written about them.

In contrast, the comparison leaders in our study—people like Al Dunlap of Scott Paper (the comparison company to Kimberly-Clark), Lee Iacocca of Chrysler (a company that failed to make a sustained shift from good to great) and Stanley Gault of Rubbermaid (a company that imploded after Gault departed)—garnered vastly more attention. Some of the comparison CEOs became wealthy celebrities—covers of magazines, bestselling autobiographies, massive compensation packages—despite the fact that their long-term results failed to measure up to the quiet, unknown Level 5s. In over two-thirds of the comparison companies, we noted the presence of a gargantuan personal ego that contributed to the demise or continued mediocrity of the company. These leaders were ambitious for themselves, and they succeeded admirably on this score, but they failed utterly in the task of creating an enduring great company.

SESSION 2: HOMEWORK SUMMARY

Due Date: _____

Review of homework assignments:

John the Baptist

© Copyright 1996 Richard L. Shepherd

You may reproduce this chapter at no charge as long as proper credit is given and no changes are made to the document

A Look at a Biblical Philosophy of Ministry

When we come to the life of John the Baptist, we come to one of the most unique men and one of the most unique ministries in all of Scripture. The announcement of his birth was supernatural. His birth was miraculous. His upbringing was extraordinary. His first months of ministry were marked by the touch of God. His proclamation of the Coming One, the Messiah, was fulfilled and more. His finish seemed surprising and tragic. What can we learn from him? What does the Scripture reveal?

1. God's Plan and Purpose:

    Read Luke 7:29-30. What do you discover about…
- Jesus' view of John:

- The people's view of John:

- The Pharisee's view of John:

    Compare the response of the people with that of the Pharisees. What do you see about the plan and purpose of God? How did John fit into that plan/purpose?

We can summarize this first thought—**God has a plan and purpose that is RIGHT.**

2. God is "The Placer"

The Greek word for God (*theos*) carries the idea of "the placer," "the one who puts in place" [from *tithemi*].

    Read John 1:6, 33 and Luke 3:2; 7:27 and summarize what you find about God's sending or "placing." [Note: The words "send" or "sent" are found 53 times in the Gospel of Joh in reference to John the Baptist or Jesus.]

SERVANT APPROACH LEADERSHIP TRAINING: Building Biblical Philosophy   (revised 2/20/223)

JOHN THE BAPTIST (CONT.)

Would you agree that we could summarize the truth of God as "Placer" with this statement:

"God sends
WHO He wants…
WHERE He wants…
WHY He wants…
HOW He wants…
WHEN He wants…
to do WHAT He wants"?

♦ Do you see any personal applications in where you are right now? Think about that and write your thoughts.

3. Our "Placement" in Life and Ministry is…

…By Grace

    Read Luke 1:15, 41-44 and record what you find about the merit of John the Baptist and why God did what God did.

…By Submission and Cooperation

    Read John 3:22-30 and summarize John's viewpoint and attitude.

John spoke of himself as the Friend of the Bridegroom. Alvah Hovey notes, "According to Jewish custom, the business of negotiating and completing a marriage was entrusted to a friend of the bridegroom and therefore, when at the wedding he heard the voice of the bridegroom conversing with the bride, he rejoiced at the successful accomplishment of the task committed to him…" [p. 107]. John was full of joy. "Not a ripple of envy passes over the mighty prophet's soul; but he is glad, with a pure and perfect goodness, that the eyes of the people are turning to the King in his beauty. He is satisfied with the joy which belongs to himself, as the friend of the bridegroom." [p. 108, Commentary on the Gospel of John in **An American Commenatry on the New Testament**.]

JOHN THE BAPTIST (CONT.)

4. Sometimes OTHERS don't understand God's way or how we fit.

- Read Luke 1:13, 15, 18-20. What was Zacharias' understanding?

- Read Matthew 3:1 and Luke 7:33-34. What did the people think?

5. Sometimes WE don't understand the way God is working or how we fit.

- Read Matthew 14:3-12 and 11:2-3. Why was John in prison? What had he done?

[Note: In Matthew 11:3 John asks *"...or shall we look for someone else?"* The Greek word is *heteron* referring to "someone else" or "another" of a ***different*** kind. He was asking "Do we look for a Messiah who acts differently, who has a different way of doing things?"]

Think of all John the Baptist had seen and heard:
The prophecies of Isaiah (40:3-5) and Malachi (3:1; 4:5-6), the announcement of his birth and prophecies about his life and ministry by the angel Gabriel to his father Zacharias, the miraculous birth through Zacharias and Elizabeth, the coming of Mary to visit Elizabeth and the filling of the Spirit for her and John in the womb (leaped for joy), his birth and Zacharias' prophecy through restored voice, his growth in the wilderness/desert regions, his dress, diet and manner, the Word of God came to him in the wilderness, he was told what and who to look for, Jesus came to him and he baptized him, saw the Spirit descend as a dove and alight on Jesus, heard the Father's Voice proclaim "This is My beloved Son in Whom I am well please, pointed to Jesus as the Lamb of God, knew more and more were coming to Jesus, rejoiced as Friend of the Bridegroom, *"He must increase, I must decrease"*...then... *"Are You the Expected One/Coming One or do we look for someone different?"*

- Read John 1:29-34 and Luke 7:11-20. What insights do you see in John's question? What did Jesus do in Luke 7:21-22?

SERVANT APPROACH LEADERSHIP TRAINING: Building Biblical Philosophy (revised 2/20/223)

JOHN THE BAPTIST (CONT.)

6. Jesus Revealed The Hidden Beatitude: *"Blessed is he who keeps from stumbling over Me."* (Luke 7:23).

The word "keeps" is Aorist Passive Subjunctive. An expanded translation would be "Blessed [*makarios* = Totally satisfied from the inside out] is he who keeps from being caused possible to stumble over Me or stumble at some point by something I do or say or the way I AM or act." Jesus is saying it is possible to stumble, but it is not necessary.

♦ Write any personal applications you see in this passage.

7. Sometimes we must wait to see how all things fit.

- Read Acts 13:25. According to this verse God had a "course" [*dromos*—a racecourse marked out] set out/placed for John to run. Did John complete his course?

- Read Acts 20:24 and 2 Timothy 4:7-8. What insights do you see from Paul about the course God has for each of His children? What applications do you see for your life? To ministry?

Pray over each of these 7 truths and ask the Lord to show His specific applications to your life.

Remember, God initiates/send in ministry in His way and for His Purposes. Trust Him.

SERVANT APPROACH LEADERSHIP TRAINING: Building Biblical Philosophy   (revised 2/20/223)

God-ordered Ministry – John the Baptist Notes

NOTE TAKING OUTLINE:

I. God has a _____ and a _____ that is right.

    Luke 7:28-30
    29 – Acknowledged God's _____ (Rightness)

    30 – Rejected God's _____

    Luke 1:5-12

    13 – When was the last time they prayed?
    18 – A Statement of _____
    19 – Sent: God-_____(Not by his great _____, but by God's ____.)

II. God sends where, when, how, who, to do what and why _____ _____.
    John 1:6 – "..._____ *from God*"
    John 1:33 – "...*He who* _____ *Me*..."
    Luke 3:1-2 – Who – the word of God came to _____

        Where – _____

        When – _____ year

    Luke 3:3-4 – Why – Make _____
    Luke 7:27 – ___send _____ Messenger

III. We can be a _____ of it:
    A. By _____

    Luke 1:15 – Filled in _____

    Luke 1:41 – Elizabeth Filled

    B. By _____

        Matt. 3:13-15 – "...*Then he* _____ *Him*"

SERVANT APPROACH LEADERSHIP TRAINING: Building Biblical Philosophy

GOD-ORDERED MINISTRY – JOHN THE BAPTIST NOTES (CONTINUED)

Luke 3:16 – "...*I am not fit...*"

John 3:22-27 – "..._____ *him from heaven*"

John 3:28 – "...*I have been* _____"

John 3:30 – He must _____ more and I must _____ more.

    C. With the _____

Luke 9:7-9 – A sense of _____ about John and Jesus – Both initiated by the Father.

John 5:22 – Jesus was sent by the _____.

John 8:13, 26, 42; 5:24, 30, 36, 37; 9:4; 12:49; 14:10; Isaiah 50

IV. Sometimes _____ don't _____ God's purpose and plan and how we fit into it.
    Luke 7:33 – "...*and you say he has a* _____"

    Luke 1:15 – They _____ how he did what he did.

    Luke 1:18 – Zacharias didn't _____.

V. Sometimes ___ don't understand this nor how we _____.

    Luke 7:18-19 – "*Are You the* _____*One?*"

    Luke 7:23 – _____ is he who keeps from _____ over Me (over the way I do things).

Summary:

We must trust the way God _____ His ministry (_____ He does _____ He does).

"*Blessed is he who keeps from stumbling over Me.*"

God-Ordered Ministry – John the Baptist Notes (continued)

Notes:

Philosophy of Church Government

© Copyright 2001 Eddie Rasnake

You may reproduce this chapter at no charge as long as proper credit is given and no changes are made to the document.

The Church belongs to God, not man. Christ said, *"upon this rock I will build MY church."* How does God want His church to be led? This is the most important question to be asked of any church – not what do we think is most efficient, but what does God desire. In 1 Peter 5 we have some clear instructions on how church leadership is to function.

Whether one is in a position of leadership or not, every believer has a vested interest in how their church is led. In this age of plurality, not only are there denominations of every imaginable style and structure, but also individual churches add even more facets and options. When it comes to leadership structure, sadly, a great many churches have evolved into their present structure, rather than designing it in an intentional manner. They are what they are by a mixture of culture and chance, tradition and timidity. And many are not what the Lord would desire. Practically speaking, Christ is not the head of many churches. They are led either by powerful people, or the personal preferences of the masses instead of by the Lord.

What Peter writes speaks volumes if we are willing to look at it closely. He tells us what leaders are called: elders. He tells us their job: shepherd the flock of God by exercising oversight. He tells us how they are motivated: not by compulsion, but voluntarily; not for sordid gain, but with eagerness. He tells us how they are guided: according to the will of God. He tells us the mistake they can make: lording it over those allotted to their charge. He tells us how they are to do their job: proving to be examples (models) to the flock. He tells us why it is worth it to lead well: eternal reward – crowns in heaven. Most importantly, he tells us how everyone, leaders **and** followers, are to be: humble, not proud. WHAT A BLUEPRINT FOR CHURCH LEADERSHIP! Yet sadly, not every church reflects this divine desire.

Before we can consider where the church ought to be, we first must consider where it is. If we know where we want to go, a key part of getting there is knowing where we are. Much like that dot you find on the map at the local mall, "You Are Here" is a very important part of being able to make it to where you want to be.

In this lesson we would like to look at the three major types of church leadership practiced today and evaluate each in the light of Scripture. We will also attempt to identify the Biblical principles that make or break any leadership style. As one looks around at the myriad of models, three dominant styles of church leadership emerge: I call them Democratic Leadership, Dictatorial Leadership, and Divine Leadership. Let's look at these one at a time and consider the Biblical support for them.

Democratic Leadership

Perhaps the most common leadership style among churches in America is the democratic model. It is also sometimes called "congregational rule." Under this model every member of the church is given a vote on the significant issues facing the church. Of course, they also get to vote on what constitutes a "significant" issue. This could be anything from the next Senior Pastor to the menu for church suppers. In such a system, the majority wins and the minority loses. What is the key to effective leadership in such a system? **POLITICS!** To get things done, one must win a majority to their way of thinking.

PHILOSOPHY OF CHURCH GOVERNMENT (CONT.)

What is the Biblical basis for such a system? The most common defense for congregational rule is what is referred to as the "priesthood" of the believer.

Look at 1 Peter 2:4-5, 9 and write down what you learn about this idea of the "priesthood" of the believer.

While this passage certainly seems to identify every Christian as a priest, it is important to realize that this does not necessarily mean that every believer has an equal say in the direction of the church. It is interesting to note that in this same context Peter goes on to say *"Submit yourselves for the Lord's sake to every human institution..."* (v.13). One of the problems of interpreting this verse to mean that every member should have an equal say in church decisions is that it misses the fact that not every member is a believer. Jesus made it clear in the parable of "the Wheat and the Tares" that there are unbelievers mixed in with believers and they will not be separated until the Lord returns. While every true believer is a priest unto God, and this means every believer is able to hear from God and follow His leading, this does not mean that every believer should have a say in every decision of a church's life. A vote simply tells us what the majority of the people want. It does not always tell us what God wants. It is interesting that in Korah's rebellion when the leadership of Moses was challenged, Korah put forward this same argument.

📖 Read Numbers 16:1-3.

What is the basis of Korah's argument against Moses' leadership?

What is God's response to Korah (see 16:31-35)?

The core argument Korah puts forward here is basically, "Why should you make all the decisions? Every one of us is holy. We can hear from God too." It is interesting that he uses the same idea as in 1 Peter 2:9, *"...a holy nation."* Korah is lobbying for a democracy. What is Moses' response to Korah's charges? The only defense he offers is *"...the Lord has sent me"* (16:28). Moses didn't consider himself more qualified than Korah. Yet he knew he was called to lead. God's verdict on Korah's counsel is clear: the ground opens up and swallows him and those who rebelled with him. Immediately after this, we have God's call on the tribe of Levi dramatically affirmed by Aaron's rod budding and blossoming and bearing fruit, a testimony that God had appointed them as the spiritual leaders of Israel. This rod was kept in the ark of the covenant as a reminder of God's answer to Korah's question.

PHILOSOPHY OF CHURCH GOVERNMENT (CONT.)

The Old Testament is replete with examples from the history of Israel when the majority of God's people were not following Him. What about this idea of majority rule?

Majority Rule in Scripture

📖 As far as I have been able to discover, I can find only two clear examples in Scripture of majority rule in a decision. Take a look at each and write what you find, reflecting on whether the majority seemed to be right or not based on the results of the decision.

Numbers 13:25-33

Acts 27:1-44 (notice the word "majority" in v.12)

In Numbers 13 we see the story of the twelve spies sent in to spy out the promised land of Canaan. When they return, their opinion is divided. The counsel of the majority (ten of the spies) is that the land is unconquerable. Only the minority of Caleb and Joshua have the mind of the Lord on the subject. As we consider the scenario in Numbers 13 we do not have to wonder whether the majority was right or not. We have the commentary of God on the subject. The majority report resulted in forty years of wandering as a consequence of Israel's unwillingness to follow God.

Likewise, when we look to the New Testament, we find a similar negative example of majority rule. We see in Paul's journey to Rome that it was the majority who overruled his wise counsel to put into port for winter, and the result was shipwreck. I wonder how many times a church has met with shipwreck because of following the will of the majority.

While the two examples we see are both negative with grave consequences, certainly God can still work through a church which makes decisions by vote and majority rule. Sometimes the majority will have the mind of God. But there is not as much protection in such a system. Think about it. If decisions are made by vote, then the vote of the minority counts for nothing, even if it is right and the will of God. If 49% have the mind of God on an issue, they can still be outvoted if 51% of the members don't. Their vote means nothing if they are in the minority.

Dictatorial Leadership

A second style of leadership we see modeled in a great many churches is dictatorial leadership. This is authoritarian rule based on the vision of one man or a small controlling body of men. In such a system, one man or one group makes all the important decisions. Everyone else either follows or rebels. In such a

PHILOSOPHY OF CHURCH GOVERNMENT (CONT.)

system, the minority controls and the majority has no vote or voice. What is the key to effective leadership in such a system? **POWER!** To get things done, one must keep control of the decision-making power in the church. Sometimes the dictator is a Senior pastor. Other times it may be a deacon board or an elder board. The title is not as defining as the function. When a select few make all the decisions (right and wrong), you have a dictatorship.

What is the Biblical basis for such a system? While few would label themselves a dictatorship, many times such a leadership style is not only the practiced reality, it is defended as spiritual when challenged. The most common defense, ironically, is the same example we looked at of Korah's rebellion. "To reject God's leader is to reject God", they argue. And yet, such an argument only works so long as the leader follows God in every decision. Even Moses was judged by God when he didn't follow the Lord's lead. In fact, he was denied the opportunity to lead Israel into the promised land because of a choice to follow himself instead of the Lord.

We see a number of examples of dictatorial style leadership in the Bible, most of them in the kings which led Israel. The most notable of these is King Saul. He was selected as king by the people, yet in giving him as a leader God was judging, rather than blessing Israel.

📖 Look at 1 Samuel 8:10-18. What did Samuel say a king with absolute power would do to Israel?

When Israel asked for a king, they wanted a strong, visible leader *"like all the nations"* (8:5). Samuel warned them that to give one man such power over them would come at a price. He mentions a number of consequences of such a system: their children would serve him, he would take some of the blessings meant for them, and they themselves would end up serving him. While pastors with such absolute power in a congregation are rare, the example of Jim Jones and the Guyana tragedy underscore that this principle, taken to an extreme, can have deadly consequences. But even where the power given to one or a few is not absolute, there can still be too much authority given without enough accountability and it can negatively affect the church. The wise words of Lord Acton are as true today as in his day: "Power corrupts, and absolute power corrupts absolutely."

It is important to recognize that any church structure can become a dictatorship in the absence of proper accountability or checks and balances. Whether it is a self-serving elder board, or a pastor with "yes men" for deacons, or a deacon chairman who no one is willing to cross or confront, or a small church dominated by its largest financial contributor – any kind of church can become a dictatorship if God's word and will ceases to be the standard for every decision. It is worth noting that in the example of King Saul God's verdict on the people was that when they chose a dictator, they were rejecting the Lord's headship over them (1 Samuel 8:7).

The Role of Culture in Leadership Style

How does a church establish its leadership style? How is the initial course maintained over the years? There are two main ways a church defines itself in terms of leadership: Either they borrow the dominant

Philosophy of Church Government (cont.)

leadership models they see in their culture, or they go directly to God's Word and try to implement what they see there. Sadly more churches seem to line up with the former approach than the latter. It is interesting to me that in America where I live, the cultural norm is democracy and that is the dominant model in the church as well. I have made some two-dozen trips to minister in the former Soviet Union and Iron Curtain areas of Europe. It may surprise you to know that in these parts of the world where for over seventy years dictatorship was the norm, most of the churches follow a dictator model. It seems that culture affects church structure more than we are willing to admit. But what does God's Word teach?

Divine Leadership

In a system of democracy, everyone has a vote, but only the voice of the majority is heard, and they are the ones who make the decisions. In a system of dictatorship, no one has a vote or voice except those who control the strings of power (which more often than not are those strings attached to the purse) and the decisions are made by a select few. But divine leadership is unique and distinct from both these styles. In divine leadership there are not decisions to be made but directions to be followed. The goal is not to decide what seems the best course, but to discern God's guiding. It really is an issue of whether man or God will have his way.

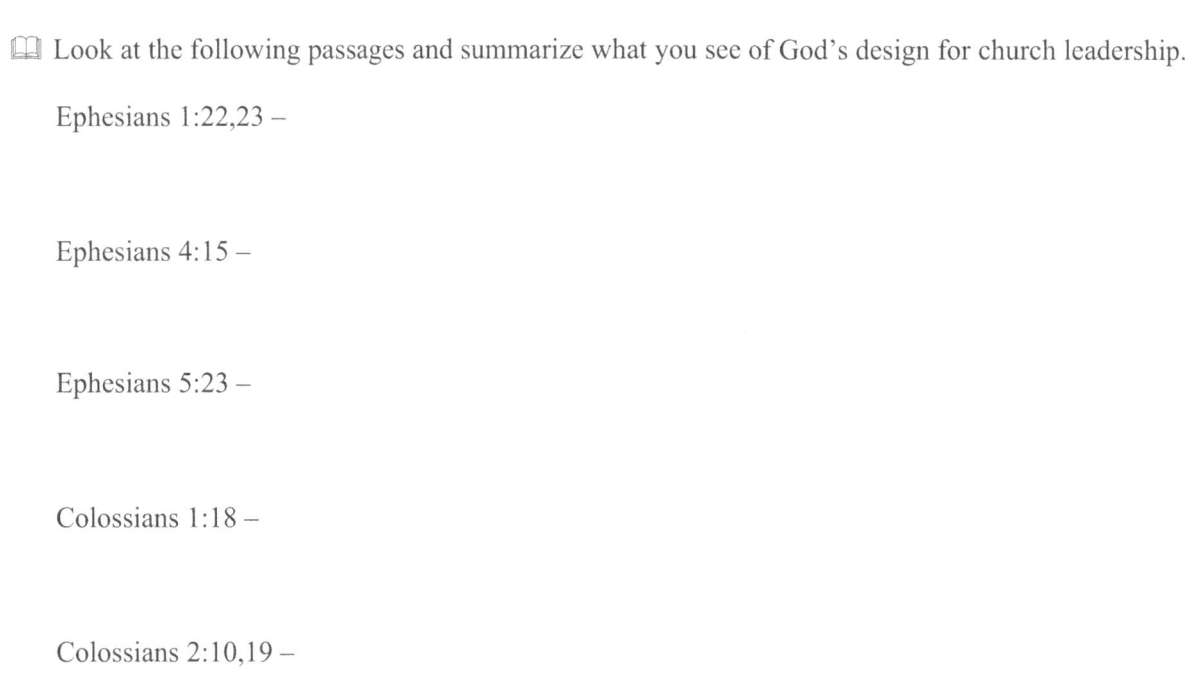

📖 Look at the following passages and summarize what you see of God's design for church leadership.

Ephesians 1:22,23 –

Ephesians 4:15 –

Ephesians 5:23 –

Colossians 1:18 –

Colossians 2:10,19 –

The New Testament is emphatic that Christ, not a pope or a pastor, is the head of the church. This is not theory it is reality. It is more than mere creed. Look at what we see in these verses. In Ephesians 1:22 Christ is defined as *"head over all things"* and in v.23 the church is defined as His *"body"*. In this picture we see a beautiful analogy of the working of the church. He is the brain, guiding and directing His hands

PHILOSOPHY OF CHURCH GOVERNMENT (CONT.)

and feet to do His work. In Ephesians 4:15 this idea is reiterated. Ephesians 5:23 states clearly, *"Christ is the head of the church."* In Colossians 1:18 this is repeated with the added emphases that He is to have first place in everything. The church is not a democracy or a dictatorship, it is a monarchy with one King – the King of Kings. In Colossians 2:10,19 we see repeated almost verbatim the ideas put forward in Ephesians. The headship of Christ is the key principle which separates the church from the world in which it exists. As Ephesians 4:4-6 puts it, *"there is one body ... one spirit ... one hope ... one Lord ... one faith ... one baptism ... one God and Father of all who is over all and through all and in all."* This is the church's leadership mandate!

But how does such a system work practically? Under divine leadership, God decides, and the church follows. How the church follows must take into account a reality we mentioned earlier – the New Testament congregation is a mixed multitude. There are believers and unbelievers. Practically, for divine leadership to be the norm and to be lived out in reality, decisions should be trusted to the most spiritually mature in the congregation. This is at the core of the elder model of leadership. Rightly done, it presupposes that a plurality of the spiritually mature should be trusted with the job of hearing from God. This plurality is to discern God's leading and then lead others to follow it.

Notice the differences between the three models we have looked at. In a democracy **POLITICS** is key. One must persuade by whatever means a majority to his way of thinking. In a dictatorship **POWER** is the key. One must have control and then exercise it. In a divine leadership model **PRAYER** is the key. God must be heard. Seeking Him becomes job #1. We see this underscored in Acts 6 – the selection of the first deacon-types – where James makes it clear that the main leaders would devote themselves to *"prayer and the ministry of the word"* (Acts 6:4).

Let's look at some Biblical examples of the principle of divine leadership in action.

- Read Acts 15:25 in its context and write what stands out to you about the idea of a group of the spiritually mature seeking God's leading.

Acts 15:25 is in the context of the "Jerusalem Council" a meeting of the main leadership of the mother church with the apostle Paul considering the question of whether a Gentile had to become a Jew to become a Christian. Verse 25 tells us some significant things about what following God as a group looks like. We see that they "became of one mind". This suggests two important points. First, the word "became" implies that they weren't of one mind in the beginning. It took time to reach agreement. Second, the phrase "of one mind" makes it clear that they eventually did come to agreement. The implication is that when they were all of the same opinion, they concluded it must be God's leading. One man could miss God's will, and even a majority could possibly be in the wrong. But when all trusted with the decision were in agreement that was a sign that God had spoken.

- Look at Titus 1:5 and make note of the instructions you find there.

PHILOSOPHY OF CHURCH GOVERNMENT (CONT.)

In Titus 1:5 the apostle Paul instructs Titus to *"appoint elders in every city"* as he had been instructed. Look at the key words here. First, he is to appoint elders. The word is plural here, just as it is every time it is used in the New Testament except when it is describing what an elder does. The New Testament always presents human leadership as a plurality. This is a protection from the fact that no one follows God's leading 100% of the time. As James puts it, *"we all stumble in many ways."* One man can miss God at a point in time, but with others around him, he has a safeguard to call him to seek again. Another key term in this verse is the word "every". Each local body needs a plural leadership team. A religious hierarchy in one place is no substitute for local leadership.

We see from both of these examples a Biblical model of a plural leadership team charged with the task of hearing from God. While I personally think elder leadership is the best model, I think it is important to separate the principle from the program. The elder principle can and does function in every different kind of church. A democratically led church can still use the principles of plurality and unanimity to protect their process. A congregationally ruled church can and should use prayer rather than politics to determine God's leading. Even a dictatorship can follow God if those in power seek the Lord. They just don't have the same protection for times of weakness or distraction. Any church is better when the leaders lay aside politics and power-plays and devote themselves to prayer and the Word (God's written will).

In conclusion, I would like to highlight two key principles we looked at that make divine leadership a reality. First, there must be plurality – this provides accountability and checks and balances. Second, there must be unanimity. If God has spoken, He has not set two different directions for the church. If there is disagreement, at least one view is the wrong one. It may even be the majority view as we saw with the 12 spies. It may be the minority report that protects the whole from a major mistake. One elder, or even one church member, who has heard from God is all the majority that is needed if all want God's will. I would like to add one final principle to what makes divine leadership become a reality. It is when the leaders see themselves as servants – as serving the congregation by seeking God. In Luke 22:24-27 Jesus set down a definition of spiritual leadership. He said, *"The kings of the Gentiles lord it over them; and those who have authority over them are called 'Benefactors.' But not so with you, but let him who is the greatest among you become as the youngest, and the leader as the servant. For who is greater, the one who reclines at the table, or the one who serves? Is it not the one who reclines at the table? But I am among you as the one who serves."* True Biblical elders (whatever their human title) serve God's people by seeking Him.

The Headship of Christ is the Biblical model and mandate for the church. It is lived out when a plurality of leaders search the Scriptures to see what God has already revealed of His will, and also seek His face to discern His direction in the decisions to be made. They must devote themselves to the word and prayer. It is not enough to walk in what the majority perceives as wisdom, for this may only be man's wisdom. Good works are not always the same as God's works. Only when there is unanimity is their confidence that God has been heard. This means Christ is the head of the local body, not the elders. True Biblical elders are merely servants – they are mature believers entrusted with the responsibility to seek God and then lead as He leads. If Christ is head of the local body, then what Scripture teaches will take precedent over "we've always done it that way" or the whims of those with control. This is what divine leadership is all about.

HOMEWORK SUMMARY

Due Date: _____

Review of homework assignments:

The 7 Pillars for a Biblical Philosophy of Ministry

© Copyright 1995 Eddie Rasnake
Associate Pastor of Discipleship, Woodland Park Baptist Church

You may reproduce this chapter at no charge as long as proper credit is given and no changes are made to the document.

Within the workings of the church there can always be found true ministry and false ministry, a valid and an invalid ministry. All valid ministry is initiated, empowered, sustained and completed by the Lord Jesus through the Holy Spirit. True ministry is always marked by righteousness and holiness (Romans 14:17; 2 Corinthians 7:1). No work (or "ministry") of the flesh is of any value in God's Kingdom (Philippians 3:3-8). The work of a man or woman of God, though he or she be beset by weakness, ignorance, and frailty in many ways (Romans 8:26) will prosper if it is a work of God (designed, initiated, empowered, and sustained by Him).

1: Initiated

True Ministry is initiated by God. Because another church or ministry does something, or someone requests a ministry is not sufficient reason for beginning a ministry. A need is not enough to justify a ministry—there must be an identifiable sense of God's leading (John 3:27-28; 1 Timothy 1:12; 1 Kings 18:36).

A ministry (or service) in the Kingdom of God is valid only as it relates properly to the King. He is the initiator of all true ministry. That is true of any kingdom. In the Gospel of John, Jesus revealed that He was "sent" by His Father (John 6:57. In John, "send" or "sent" is used 53 times referring to Jesus or John the Baptist). John the Baptist spoke of being sent by God (John 3:28) and testified that Jesus was sent by God (John 3:34). Jesus sent His disciples out as He had been sent (John 20:21).

It is the same in all the history of the church. God, the Righteous King, sends His people to minister in His Name and by His Authority, power, enablement, direction, and for His glory and the sake of His Kingdom. John the Baptist understood this (John 3:26-35). Luke testified of this in describing the ministry direction given to Paul in Acts 16:6-10. The record in Acts reveals that the Holy Spirit initiated the ministry of Barnabas and Saul/Paul (Acts 13:2) and the ministry of the Ephesian elders (Acts 20:28). In Colossians 4:17, Paul told Archippus to "take heed to the ministry which you have *received* in the Lord."

 📖 In 1 Kings 18 we read the story of Elijah challenging the prophets of Baal on Mount Carmel. Take a moment to read the chapter to remind yourself of the details. List the verses that speak of God initiated ministry and what they say.

7 PILLARS (CONTINUED)

2: Anointed

What God initiates, He anoints. When God raises up a ministry, there will be His supply and results for that ministry. Where God guides, He provides (Genesis 48:15). If God is not providing what is necessary (money, personnel, etc.), we must ask if we are where He is guiding. When God initiates ministry according to His desire and design, He also is the one who empowers, sustains, and strengthens His servants for that ministry. Paul clearly spoke of this in Colossians 1:29. The Lord is the source of our strength for the walk and warfare of our service in the Kingdom (Ephesians 6:10-20). He holds us responsible to *rely upon* Him and to obey and fulfill what He calls us to do. In Colossians 4:17, Archippus was told to "fulfill" the ministry he received from the Lord.

- Looking back at Elijah on Mount Carmel, make a list of everything that gives evidence of something God has anointed.

3: Received

True Ministry is received, not achieved. Even when we have a sense that something is God's will, it may not be His timing. Often there is a period of waiting between our awareness of a need and God raising up His solution. We are responsible to *wait* on the Lord in faith until He gives direction, and then *act* in faith on that direction (Colossians 4:17; Acts 20:24). What is not of faith is sin—missing the mark (Romans 14:23). We can be assured that when He gives direction there is peace because the wisdom from above is peaceable. When there is strife and disorder, one can know He has not spoken and that waiting is needed (James 3:13-18). Paul refused to listen to or depend on the flesh (Philippians 3:3-8; Galatians 5:16-17) and chose to walk by faith in all of life and ministry (Philippians 3:9-21; 4:1; Galatians 2:20-21; 5:22-25) depending on the Lord's leading and empowering (Colossians 1:29; Ephesians 6:10).

- Compare 1 Kings 18:1 with James 5:16-18 and write down whether you think Elijah's prayer was "achieved" (something manufactured) or "received" (something God gave him to do).

7 PILLARS (CONTINUED)

4: Surrendered

True Ministry is not the result of commitment, but surrender. Ministry that flows out of man's efforts requires striving and matters not in eternity. Ministry that flows out of surrender requires continual yieldedness and lasts for eternity (Romans 12:1-2; Ephesians 5:18).

Paul balances God's empowering with our labor in 1 Corinthians 3:8-15 by speaking of the fact that (1) God is the source of all life and growth in our Kingdom labors, and (2) He holds us responsible for the kind of labor we do. The gold, silver, and precious stones speak of that which comes from His righteous working in and through the believer. The wood, hay, and stubble represent the workings of the flesh even as it does in Jeremiah 23:16-32. There, God compares the ministry of those who speak out of their own imagination (initiated by a fleshly mind) as furnishing the people "straw" rather than good grain (Jeremiah 23:28). Their "ministry" failed to furnish the people "the slightest benefit" (Jeremiah 23:32).

> You could legitimately divide the religious experience of the apostle Paul into two categories: striving and surrender. Take a look at Philippians 3:3-9 and identify all the "credentials" that came from Paul's years of striving.

What was Paul's attitude toward the things he had "achieved?"

> What does Philippians 4:13 indicate about the way Paul accomplished his ministry?

5: Glorifies

God gets the glory. Ministry that flows out of man's efforts glorifies man. Ministry that flows out of surrender glorifies God who does the work and brings the results (1 Peter 4:10-11).

All ministry is for the sake of the King and His Kingdom. In Matthew 6:10 Jesus taught His disciples to pray *"Your Kingdom come, Your will be done on earth as it is in heaven."* God is to get the glory for all He does. First Corinthians 3:21 reminds us that no one should boast *in men* and 1 Corinthians 1:29 says *"no man may boast before God."* Let all boasting be done about the Lord and His work (1 Corinthians 1:31). Romans 11:33-36 reveals this and concludes in one sweeping declaration that *"from Him and through Him and to Him are all things. To Him be the glory forever. Amen."* It is the will of God that each member of the Body of Christ live and serve in this way.

SERVANT APPROACH LEADERSHIP TRAINING: Building Biblical Philosophy (revised 2/20/223)

7 PILLARS (CONTINUED)

📖 Look at Romans 15:17,18 and identify the things of which Paul would and would not boast.

6: Organism

True ministry is an organism, not an organization. A true ministry that is of the Lord is like a living organism, not simply a programmed organization. Because of this, the traditional business model of structure, leadership, and programs not only will not always succeed, but often will hinder the working of the Lord (1 Corinthians 12:12-14; Romans 12:4-5).

📖 Read Ephesians 4:15,16 and identify what is said there about how the church is to grow.

7: Equipping

The role of church leadership is not to do all the work of service, but to equip the laity for their works of service in and through the Body of Christ. It is the laity who carry the load of the work of the church (Ephesians 4:11-12; Hebrews 13:20-21; 2 Timothy 3:16-17). The only spectators in the Christian life are those who have finished the race (Hebrews 12:1-4).

📖 In Ephesians 4:11,12 identify who the leaders are, what their job is, and who is to do the *"work of service."*

7 Pillars (Continued)

Notes:

Philosophy of Ordination

© Copyright 1998 Eddie Rasnake

You may reproduce this chapter at no charge as long as proper credit is given and no changes are made to the document.

Before one can see how the ordination of a man to the ministry to which God has called him fits within the workings of a local church, they must first understand the philosophy of ministry and the four distinctives of ministry. Review *Seven Pillars for a Philosophy of Ministry* and *The Ministry Distinctives of WPBC*.

Observations

TO CALL

The man and the ministry given by God are to be marked by the order and fruit that God designed for the local church and its ministries (1 Timothy 3:15). With the understanding that true ministry is *received*, not *achieved*, that it is God and not man who initiates the ministry of an individual or a church, one can begin to understand where he fits in God's design and better see His call.

 📖   Read Acts 13:2-4; 16:9,10; Romans 1:1; and Galatians 1:15.
- What different Greek words are used for "call" in these verses, and what are their tense/voice/mood/part-of-speech?

- What is significant in their differences? What significance does their tense/voice/mood have?

A true minister is "called" by God before he is hired by a church or an organization, but God's calling of him is evidenced fully and finally through God providing him with a ministry. Since true ministry is empowered by God, not man, true ministry cannot be the result of education. It comes from the transformation that God works in an individual. Therefore, a college or seminary degree does not in itself qualify one for ordination, nor does the lack of it make one disqualified. True ministry is not the result of man's striving or of human effort and strategy, but of God's moving and working in and through an individual's life. Because of this, all ministers are responsible to God for their faithful service. Although people may glorify a man for what God does through him, it is the responsibility of the servant of God to do everything in his power to draw attention away from himself and focus it on God.

PHILOSOPHY OF ORDINATION (CONTINUED)

TO ORDAIN

The New Testament clearly indicates that the minister of God is uniquely set apart or appointed to his office. The term normally used for the appointing of a minister or church leader in the New Testament is **kathistemi** (Strong's #2525), which means "to ordain." The concept of ordination implies official recognition by the leadership of the church and a public announcement setting men aside for special ministry.

📖 Look up the meaning for *kathistemi* and write down the definition:

LAYING ON HANDS

The Biblical models suggest that a part of this process involves "the laying on of hands" by the existing church leadership. This New Testament practice takes its meaning from the Old Testament.

📖 Read Genesis 48:14,15; Leviticus 3:2; 24:10-15; Numbers 27:15-21; Deuteronomy 34:9; Acts 8:14-17; 19:6; 1 Timothy 4:14; and Hebrews 6:2.
Answer the following questions for each passage:

- Who did the laying on of hands?

- On whom did they lay their hands?

- Where did they lay their hands?

- Where did this activity take place?

- What was the purpose of the laying on of hands?

- What is different in this passage from the other passages? What is the same? What is the significance of the difference or similarity?

The Old Testament sacrificial system used the laying of hands on the sacrifice as a means of "identifying" with it so its payment could be experienced vicariously. The laying on of hands therefore became a means by which one could identify himself with another. The New Testament ordination demonstrates identification by the church leadership with the one on whom hands are laid. It serves as a stamp of approval if you will, a visible means of saying, "We commend you to the ministry of God. We stand with you, we support you, and affirm your right to function in a position of leadership." We see this demonstrated in Acts 13:2-3, 14:26 and 15:40 in the life and ministry of Paul.

Philosophy of Ordination (Continued)

Because this commendation and affirmation, if done with integrity, requires more than a cursory knowledge of the one being ordained, it is appropriate and right that the sending church, not the calling church, does the ordination as they will have had the time for thorough oversight and proving of the individual. This need is emphasized in Paul's exhortation to Timothy, *"Do not lay hands upon anyone too hastily and thereby share responsibility for the sins of others"* (1 Timothy 5:22). This speaks strongly of the seriousness of ordination. This seriousness is further emphasized by the fact that when the apostles appointed the first elders (Acts 14:23) the decision was preceded by *"having prayed with fasting."*

The Process

The beginning point of the calling of God is *thirsting*. First Timothy 3:1 says, *"...if any man aspires to the office of overseer, it is a fine work he desires to do."* The calling of God begins with a longing, a thirsting to be used in His service.

The next step in the process is *training*. The New Testament makes it clear that ministry is no different than any other profession in its need for training and preparation. Ephesians 4:11-12 tells us that saints need to be *"equipped"* for the work of service. Any called man must go through a time of preparation to sharpen his usefulness. This process doesn't stop with ordination, but there is a defined level of acceptability.

The third step in the process is *testing*. The called man, concurrent with his training, should have opportunity to be tested in his service. He should prove himself for a time serving under the leadership of others. This should also include evaluation. (see 1 Timothy 3:10).

Finally, once he has shown himself *"approved"* (see 2 Timothy 2:15), there comes a point of *trusting*, where, by the commendation of the sending church, he is entrusted to the ministry God has called him to by his ordination.

- Read Acts 6:1-8; Exodus 18:13-27; and Deut. 1:9-18. Create a consolidated list of characteristics a leader should have.

Ordination to the Gospel Ministry is a matter of great significance both in the life of the local church and in the life of the man being set apart for this ministry. In essence it is a recognition that God's calling and gifts have been given to a man for the purpose of proclaiming the truth of the Word of Jesus Christ, a calling of eternal significance, impact, and reward.

PHILOSOPHY OF ORDINATION (CONTINUED)

Ordination at WPBC

As we noted previously, 1 Timothy 5:22 points out the seriousness of this matter when it commands not to lay hands on a person *"too hastily."* In light of this, the following guidelines apply to the matter of ordination at Woodland Park:
The individual must...
- Give testimony and show evidence of being born again (John 3:3,5-8; Titus 3:4-7; 1 Peter 1:22-23) and show a consistent and maturing walk with the Lord (1 Timothy 3:6; 4:15-16).

Show a predictability in his life in line with the qualifications of elders/pastors found in 1 Timothy 3:1-7; Titus 1:6-9; 1 Peter 5:1-3. (Complete the "Character Qualifications Questionnaire," as well as read the Appendix to *The Constitution and Bylaws of Woodland Park*).

- Agree to the doctrinal statement found in *The Constitution of Woodland Park*.
- Agree with the "Philosophy of Ministry" statement of Woodland Park.
- Agree with the "Philosophy of Ordination" statement.
- Give evidence of calling (being sent), burden, and giftedness for ministry as well as the receiving of a specific ministry (Romans 12:6-8; John 3:27-28; Col. 4:17).
- When a person has given evidence of the above qualifications he may be considered for ordination at Woodland Park. The procedure is as follows:
    a) Sign a statement of agreement with the position statements given above.
    b) Complete the Ordination Questionnaire (to be completed, typed, and handed in before an Ordination Council date is set).
    c) At least 3 Personal Reference Questionnaires must be received. Once items a), b) and c) have been completed, a date is set for an Ordination Council.
    d) Meet with the Ordination Council for a time of testimony and affirmation.
- After approval by the Ordination Council the ordination will take place in one of the worship services of Woodland Park.

SESSION 4: HOMEWORK SUMMARY

Due Date: _____

Review of homework assignments:

Philosophy of Evangelism

© Copyright 1996 Eddie Rasnake

You may reproduce this chapter at no charge as long as proper credit is given and no changes are made to the document.

Predestination vs. Free Will

It is impossible to address the subject of evangelism properly without addressing the controversy of predestination verses free will, for this poses a great problem in establishing a working philosophy. In the truest sense however, it is not the two separate doctrines that pose a problem, but rather, that people continue to debate how to reconcile the two. By establishing debate and drawing battle lines, the inevitable result is one group that lays hold of the truths of predestination and sovereignty while attempting to explain away texts that teach a person's responsibility. Another group is produced which clings tightly to free will and either ignores or attempts to explain away the Biblical doctrine of sovereignty in evangelism. Neither group is correct. Clearly the Bible teaches both God's sovereignty and human responsibility. While it is a mystery *how* God accomplishes both of these doctrines, the truth of them must be accepted as reality. In Romans 11, using the analogy of the olive tree, Paul gives a clear teaching of sovereignty. In chapter 10 he defines human responsibility as he states, *"Whoever will call upon the name of the Lord will be saved"* (Rom. 10:13). In Chapter 9 he acknowledges the question of how both can be true. But instead of answering the question, he questions the question: *"On the contrary, who are you, O man, who answers back to God"* (Rom. 9:20)? The two doctrines are an antinomy. They are not ours to reconcile. Only an all-powerful God is able to accomplish one without sacrificing the integrity of the other. That finite humans cannot reconcile the two doctrines should serve to elevate our view of and appreciation for God's sovereignty.

We must recognize that holding onto one doctrine while dismissing the other is wrong theology. Doing this inevitably leads to wrong application in evangelism. Sovereignty that excludes responsibility presents the temptation to lose sight of our God-given responsibility as ambassadors for Christ. This leads to apathy instead of empathy for the unconverted. On the other hand, responsibility that excludes sovereignty presents the temptation to take upon ourselves the job, not only of proclaiming salvation, but also of producing converts. Success or failure thus becomes defined not by faithfulness but by results. If results are not forthcoming then a person's technique is faulted, re-examined and revised until results are produced (even if they are only short-term results). Only holding both the doctrines of God's sovereignty and of man's responsibility can produce a balanced understanding of our role (and God's) in the evangelization of the world. Charles Spurgeon was once asked if he could reconcile the two doctrines to each other. "I wouldn't try," he replied. "I never reconcile friends." These truths, being Biblically affirmed, are not enemies, nor uneasy neighbors; they are friends, and they work together.

What is the Gospel?

GOD

It is first **a message about God**. The gospel tells us who He is, what He is like, what His standards are, and what He expects of us, His creation. This is the first step in the gospel process. Nothing can be accomplished in talking about sin, its consequence, and its forgiveness until one understands God's affection for and sovereignty over us. There is a potential for error here in that we may find ourselves giving an incomplete picture of God. We err if we only present the love of God. This produces a message of sloppy benevolence having no regard for the standards and expectations of a holy God. We also err if

Philosophy of Evangelism (Continued)

we only present the holiness of God. This produces a harsh accountability to God without relationship. We must present a full view of God.

Sin

Second, the gospel is **a message about sin**. It reveals each person's deficiency and rebellion; that we fall short of God's standards and expectations. Persons choose to go their own way in disregard of God's way. As such, we are deserving of God's wrath. The message also reveals that we sin because we are by nature sinners. One will not respond rightly to the message of Christ, nor will he or she see the need for it, until one understands and accepts the message of sin. There is a potential for error here as well, in that every life has something to be ashamed of in action or attitude, but this is only one facet of sin. It must also be recognized that part of our sin is not just that we have violated God's standards, but that we have failed to relate rightly with Him, our Creator.

Christ

Third, the gospel is **a message about Christ**. This message is two-fold: who He is, and what He has done. Who is Christ?

- **Incarnation**: First, we must look at His incarnation—*He is God* incarnate. He is not, nor ever claimed to be, simply a teacher or an example.

- **Atonement**: Second, we must look at His atonement—*He is Savior*. Saving faith does not simply trust the atonement. It trusts the Christ who atoned.

- **Ascension**: Third, we must look at His ascension—*He is Lord*. There is no partial atonement. We cannot confess our specific sinful actions while failing to acknowledge our failure to give God His rightful place in our life.

- **Resurrection**: Weaving through all of these is His resurrection—the Father's proof that Jesus is *God, Savior and Lord*, and that His righteous death provided full forgiveness of sin and justification before God.

Humanity

Fourth, the gospel is **a message about humanity**. Will they walk in rebellion to God, their Creator, Savior and Lord, or will they walk in relationship with Him? The message of God and sin and Christ is a message to be believed, but it is not merely a message to be believed. The two components are *repentance* (a turning from our work and our way) and *faith* (trusting in His work). Faith alone is not saving faith, for if one is unwilling to accommodate his or her life to God, one doesn't really believe in the Biblical truth of God. It must also be said that repentance alone is not saving faith. Turning from our sins has no power in itself. Otherwise, we would have no need for a savior.

Why Do We Share the Gospel?

What is our motivation for sharing the gospel? Really, there are two reasons, expressed beautifully in the Great Commandment. First, we are to love God. Love of God constrains us to obey His command and commission. He has called us as ambassadors and committed to us the message of reconciliation. We cannot say that we love Him if we do not take seriously what He says and act on His revealed will. Further, we ascribe to Him the glory He is due every time we speak of His mighty works. The second motivation, also found in the Great Commandment, is that we are to love our neighbor. Our neighbor has no greater need than salvation. Love of my neighbor will prevent me from viewing evangelism as a task or a project. It also implies that evangelism should flow through relationship.

Philosophy of Evangelism (Continued)

How Does the Church Share the Gospel?

📖 Read John 3:1 through 4:42 and answer the following questions:

1. Jesus reached out to two individuals. Make a chart showing how they were different from each other (e.g., socially, educationally, ethnically, etc.).

2. *How* did each person's background factor into the message that Christ presented them?

3. Examine the end of each conversation and notice how each of them ends. What is similar about both endings?

How does the Church share the Gospel? First, it must be recognized that evangelism is not the only task the Lord has given to us, nor will we all participate in that task in the same way. Our gifts are sovereignly bestowed, as are our opportunities to minister and the results of those opportunities. But all of us are ambassadors. An inevitable result of following Him is that He makes us fishers of men. A second recognition we must make is that the role of church leadership is not to do all the work of service, but to equip the laity. It is they, the laity, who carry the load of the work of a local church. The only spectators in the Christian life are those who have finished the race (Hebrews 12:1-4). What should this equipping look like?

📖 Read Mark 4:1-20 and answer the following questions:
1. What are the three symbols in this parable?

2. What does each symbol represent?

3. What does the sower know or do that influences the harvest?

4. How does this passage compare with 1 Cor. 3:5-9

What is Evangelism?

Louis Sperry Chafer in his "Systematic Theology" defines evangelism in this way: "…the act of presenting to the unsaved the evangel or good news of the gospel of God's saving grace through Christ Jesus." This working definition is a good place to start. First, it reminds us that evangelism is an "act of presenting." It is an action, not a result. Evangelism takes place every time the good news is presented regardless of the response, the circumstances, or the method. Bill Bright defined evangelistic success in this way: "successful witnessing is simply taking the initiative to share Christ in the power of the Holy Spirit and leaving the results to God." Results must be left in the hands of God's sovereignty. Second, Chafer's definition reminds us that evangelism is communicating a message, a message that is both good and news. There is an implication here, namely that with the message there is a specific application. This is the fulcrum upon which the human role and God's role meet. A saved person has the God-given

PHILOSOPHY OF EVANGELISM (CONTINUED)

privilege and responsibility to communicate the message of the gospel to the unsaved mind. God alone, however, is able to convict the application of the message to the unsaved heart and will.
The believer errs when he or she attempts to take upon themselves the role that is God's alone. We also err when we leave to God a role that has been delegated to us in God's revealed word.

- **Message vs. Method**: It is message focused, not method focused: Evangelism methods, no matter how effective they have been in the past or in other situations, are merely cultural packaging of the message about God, about sin, about Christ, and about humanity.

- **Lifestyle vs. Program**: It is lifestyle focused, not program focused. The most revealing component about the evangelistic impact of a church is not what happens in services or in organized activities, but what happens in the home, in the neighborhood, in the workplace, and in the day-to-day course of life. Programs may play a role, but they are never central.

- **Person vs. System**: It emphasizes trusting the person and work of Christ, not a system or plan of salvation. Our trust is not to be simply in the message of the cross, nor in the cross, but in Christ who's cross it is.

- **Process vs. Point**: Evangelism must be seen as a process, not a point. Evangelism begins with the truth about God and builds from there. The four component truths of the gospel message (God, sin, Christ, humanity) are built layer by layer. Although specific points punctuate this process, it is nonetheless a process. It includes cultivating the soil, sowing the seed of the Word, harvesting the fruit, and caring for those who believe. This process does not begin nor end at the point of initial justification. In a sense, evangelism is a component of the discipleship process and discipleship is a continuance of the evangelism process.

- **Conviction vs. Convincing**: It is the Conviction of the Holy Spirit, not the Convincing of the evangelist that saves. Humans have no power to save themselves, nor are we able to save anyone else. By God's gracious choice He allows us to join Him in His work of bringing salvation. A response to human persuasion without responding to God's conviction will not save. These conversions will not last, for "a sow, after washing, returns to wallowing in the mire." Unless there is a change of nature, a change of behavior will not last.

PHILOSOPHY OF EVANGELISM (CONTINUED)

Notes:

Philosophy of Discipleship

© Copyright 1995 Eddie Rasnake

You may reproduce this chapter at no charge as long as proper credit is given and no changes are made to the document.

Before **reading this philosophy, please answer the questions on this and the next page:**

- Use a concordance search to list all the verses in Scripture that contain the word "discipleship."

- Use a concordance search and count how many times the terms "disciple" or "disciples" appear in Scripture.

- Use a concordance search and count how many times the terms "Christian" or "Christians" appear in Scripture.

- What do you think is significant about what you learned from your concordance search?

- The Biblical term "disciple" is translated from the Greek word *mathetes* (3101). Using a Greek Dictionary, look up this word and write a summarized definition below:

- Examine John 15:7-8 and identify each of the characteristics listed here that "prove" one is a disciple. Next to each write what you think they mean.
  1.

  2.

  3.

  4.

  5.

Philosophy of Discipleship (Continued)

📖 Using your Greek tools, identify which verb in Matthew 28:18-20 is the central imperative, and which are participles that modify it, writing your observations on what this means.

📖 Examine 2 Timothy 2:2 and identify each level of ministry identified there and any differences you see between them.

The Dilemma

There is a lot of talk today about the subject of discipleship. There are a great many churches who have someone on their church staff whose job title is "Discipleship." And yet, there is very little consensus on exactly what that means, let alone, how it should express itself. Those committed to discipleship (however they define it) have a tendency to look down their noses at those who don't see its place and importance as they define it. Those who don't come from a discipleship perspective tend to tolerate those who do and view their activities as an acceptable "add-on" to the ministry of the church. They do not, however, place discipleship as the essential priority of the church. They view it as merely one of many elective activities in the church program. Before the two groups can reach a common ground, there must be a unified perspective on the definition and role of discipleship in the church. If we can agree that the Bible is the authoritative voice for defining discipleship and for identifying discipleship's role in the life of the local church, then a consensus should be within reach.

A Biblical Definition of Discipleship

The term "discipleship" does not appear in Scripture. It is a human creation in an attempt to identify the process of disciple-making. "Disciple," however, is a thoroughly Biblical term occurring over 270 times in the English translation of the Scriptures (NASB). The difference is significant. The easiest mistake to make in defining discipleship would be to do so solely by the process instead of by the product. Scripture does, I believe, communicate a sense of process both through its instruction and its models. But the trap we must watch out for is the temptation to miss the proverbial forest for the trees. In other words, we must be careful not to become so focused on a particular component that we miss the big picture. In painting a Biblical portrait of discipleship, we should begin by answering the question, "What is a disciple?"

PHILOSOPHY OF DISCIPLESHIP (CONTINUED)

What is a Disciple?

The Biblical term "disciple" is translated from the Greek word (*mathetes*) which literally means "a learner, or pupil." In the culture of the day, it communicated the idea of one who linked themselves as a follower of a recognized teacher. The word infers an intellectual process that directly shapes the lifestyle of the person. It is not an exclusively Christian term, and even in the Bible it is used of the "disciples" of John the Baptist (Mt. 11:2), of the Pharisees (Mark 2:18), and of Moses (Jn. 9:28).

Although we have clarified the terms "discipleship" and "disciple" we should now address the question "What does it mean to be a disciple of Jesus?" Scripture answers this question in several places. First, in John 15:7-8 (NASB) we read, *"If you abide in Me, and My words abide in you, ask whatever you wish, and it will be done for you. My Father is glorified by this, that you bear much fruit, and so prove to be My disciples."* These verses identify five characteristics of a disciple:

- One *abides in Christ*. A disciple is one who abides in Christ, consistently walking with Him; not perfection, but pursuit.
- The *Words of Christ* abide in them. Colossians 3:16 says, *"Let the word of Christ richly dwell within you..."*. For a disciple, the Word is his or her authority and the Word is his or her delight.
- **Prayer and answers characterize the life**. This is built on the foundation of the first two characteristics and implies a lifestyle of communion and communication with God.
- He or She *bears fruit*. Fruit is the logical consequence of the other three practices and is expressed in the fruit of Christian character (Gal.5:22-23, Mt.3:8) and the fruit of Christian ministry (Rom. 1:13, 15:28; Col. 1:10).
- He or She *glorifies God*. When a disciple abides in Christ and the words of Christ fill their life, when their life is characterized by answered prayer and fruit-bearing, they brings glory to God.

  Examine the verses below and write down how they define Biblical "fruit:"

- Galatians 5:22-23

- Matthew 3:8

- Romans 1:13

- Romans 15:28

- Colossians 1:10

Another place that addresses what it means to be a disciple is Matthew 28:18-20, which states, *"And Jesus came up and spoke to them, saying, 'All authority has been given to Me in heaven and on earth. Go therefore and make disciples of all the nations, baptizing them in the name of the Father and the Son and the Holy Spirit, teaching them to observe all that I commanded you; and lo, I am with you always, even to the end of the age.'"*

The product of disciple-making, according to this passage, is people who have identified themselves with the Lord (baptized) and who *observe all that Christ commanded*. In other words, a disciple is characterized by *identity **with** and obedience **to** Christ*. Now that we understand what a disciple is Biblically speaking, we can begin to define the process of making disciples.

PHILOSOPHY OF DISCIPLESHIP (CONTINUED)

Common Mistakes in Discipleship

ERROR #1: EXCLUDING THE LOCAL CHURCH

In modern Christianity, sadly, much of what is called discipleship is taking place outside the ministry of the local church. Yet, the Great Commission clearly identifies that the central task for the whole of the body of Christ is to "*make disciples of all the nations . . .*" Why should the local church be at the center of this task? Jesus commands that we are to be "*baptizing them in the name of the Father and the Son and the Holy Spirit.*" To "baptize" means to identify with God and implies identification with the people of God. Most discipleship-focused ministries do not baptize because they recognize this to be the responsibility of the local church. Yet clearly, Jesus includes this in the task of disciple-making. Therefore, discipleship that does not integrate local church involvement and identification is incomplete and inadequate. All the teaching and inferences of the New Testament make it clear God desires to work through His agent, the church.

ERROR #2: DISCIPLESHIP EQUALS SMALL GROUPS

One common mistake we tend to make is in how we define discipleship. A common, but flawed definition making the rounds today is that discipleship equals small groups. Let's examine this. The "discipleship = small groups" people always point to the example of Jesus and say, "See, He had twelve disciples." The problem with this statement is not in its inaccuracy, but in its incompleteness. While clearly Jesus spent a significant amount of time with the twelve, He also ministered in much broader ways. His ministry included the seventy He involved in training and ministry (Luke 10), the hundred and twenty gathered in the upper room for prayer (Acts 1), and the 5,000+ He fed who were part of His teaching ministry (Luke 9).

Many of these the Bible clearly identifies as disciples of Jesus. If discipleship equals small groups, then we are defining in terms of the process (small groups) instead of the product (those who abide in Christ, in His Word, in prayer, in fruit-bearing and in obedience). Small groups are a very useful tool in the toolbox of the disciple-maker, but there are other tools as well. A tunnel vision view of discipleship, as only small groups, guarantees that others view it as one of many programs of the church. This will not place disciple-making at the heart of the church where it belongs.

ERROR #3: SMALL GROUPS EQUALS DISCIPLESHIP

Related to the mistake of saying that discipleship equals small groups is the erroneous idea that small groups equal discipleship. Just because a group is small does not mean that it is producing disciples. Disciple-making has a clear product in view: those who abide in Christ, in His Word, in prayer, in fruit-bearing and in obedience. If what happens in the small group is not intentionally moving people in the direction of being a disciple as Scripture defines it, then discipleship is not happening regardless of what we call it. Again, we see that the product, not just the process, defines discipleship.

One of the unfortunate consequences of the tunnel vision view of those who say that discipleship equals small groups or that small groups equal discipleship is the tendency to devalue the ministries of the church other than small groups. Yet clearly, there are many things that the local church can and should do which work toward the product of making disciples. Effective Bible teaching is an important component to help people grow as obedient disciples of Jesus. Personal involvement in ministry is another component that is not limited to small group times. One-to-one counseling can fulfill an important role in discipleship. Fellowship rightly done contributes to spiritual growth. Times of corporate worship fit into the equation of disciple-making. While small groups can and should be an important tool in the toolbox, we err when we limit discipleship to that one ingredient.

PHILOSOPHY OF DISCIPLESHIP (CONTINUED)

ERROR #4: SINGLE-SOURCE MENTORING

Another common mistake we tend to make in defining discipleship is to focus on the role of the individual while neglecting the role of the environment. Again, "discipleship-by-individual" folks tend to point to Jesus to defend their view. They say, "Jesus personally discipled the twelve," and equate that with their own discipleship. Discipleship by individual is great if your discipler is Jesus, but when it is someone else, problems arise. Jesus said in Luke 6:40 that every disciple, after he or she had been fully trained, would be like their teacher. If your teacher is Jesus that works fine, but everyone else is imperfect, flawed, and stained by sin. If there is only one dominant spiritual influencer in your life, you will begin to reflect not only their strengths but also their weaknesses. Second, no one individual possesses all the spiritual gifts. It is these principles that make the small group as important as one-on-one times, and the whole environment of the church as important as the small group.

ERROR #5: IGNORING THE ENVIRONMENT

The Greenhouse Strategy

God chooses to relate to His people both corporately and individually. Discipleship that focuses only on the individual is incomplete and inadequate. God intends for the individual to be integrated into the body of Christ, both locally and universally. A family (a plural unit with mother, father, and siblings) is the God-designed unit for shaping an individual from birth to personal maturity. In the same way, the body of Christ is the God-designed unit for shaping an individual from spiritual birth to spiritual maturity. What Jesus was as an individual in terms of ministry, the church is as an entity. This is why disciple-making should be at the heart of all that a church is and all that it does. Everything ought to focus on the product of the disciple. In essence the church ought to function as a "spiritual greenhouse." In a greenhouse, everything is focused on creating the optimum environment for growth, and the individual plant is central in the design of everything.

A greenhouse is designed to provide optimum sunlight, optimum temperature, optimum humidity, optimum nutrition, optimum soil content and density, etc. It is a planned environment created so that growth happens more naturally, more rapidly and ultimately with greater quality than that of the plant left to the randomness of nature. The church ought to function in the same way. Every component of the design of the church ought to be intentional, not accidental. Everything the church is and does ought to be defined by the desired product of Biblical disciples. Programs of the church should not exist simply because "we've always done it that way," but should be intentionally designed, maintained, and modified so that growing disciples are the product. In fact, the programs will be different from place to place, from age group to age group, and from culture to culture, but the desired product will still be the same.

Where do small groups fit into the "spiritual greenhouse" we are building? To answer this, we must first recognize an important Biblical reality: all small groups are not created equal. Scripture identifies at least four different types of small groups. Obviously, Jesus and the twelve is one form of small group. As you look at the big picture it is obvious that this model was never intended to be the means of discipling everyone. This type of group was exclusive, not inclusive. Jesus said "no" to certain persons being a part of this group.

It was to be a "mentoring group" which served to develop leaders. Jesus recognized that the best way to minister to the masses was to multiply Himself into the lives of a select few who could help shoulder the burden of ministry. A second type of small group was "ministry groups." In Luke 10 when Jesus sends out the seventy, he does so by twos. These small groups included both training and practical ministry. A third type of group is what I would call "mixing groups." These groups blended the body together

Philosophy of Discipleship (Continued)

through nurturing relationships and Christ-centered fellowship. In Acts 2:46 it is said of the first century church that "...*breaking bread from house to house, they were taking their meals together with gladness and sincerity of heart.*" We know that this had to be a small group function, for the Jerusalem church at this point numbered at least three thousand (Acts 2:41) plus a hundred and twenty (Acts 1:15) and definitely all of these would not fit in one house. A fourth type of group is "missions groups" that served to expand the ministry of a local church outside its location. This is exemplified in the sending out of Paul and company from the church at Antioch on their mission journeys (Acts 13).

Mentoring groups focus on leadership, while ministry groups focus on training. Mixing groups focus on nurturing, while missions groups have a task focus. Each type of small group fills a different purpose in the greenhouse. Importantly, all these small group types are simply some of the components of the whole environment. In addition to these types of small groups, other components include large group gatherings for some of the same functions. In the modern local church, gatherings of all sizes for purposes as broad as teaching, worship, fellowship, prayer, etc. make up the toolbox of ministry. All of these tools, when they are initiated and anointed by God and when they are staffed and managed by God-gifted, God-called, and God-burdened individuals, will serve to make the local body function as the spiritual greenhouse it was intended to be. The resulting product will be growing, maturing disciples.

Structure of the Disciple-making Church

One of the factors which determines where the different types of small groups fit as well as where the other components come into play is recognizing the different levels of the discipleship process. In 2 Timothy 2:2 the apostle Paul exhorts Timothy, "*The things which you have heard from me in the presence of many witnesses, entrust these to faithful men who will be able to teach others also.*" In this statement we see reflected four generations of disciples at four different levels of maturity and ministry function.

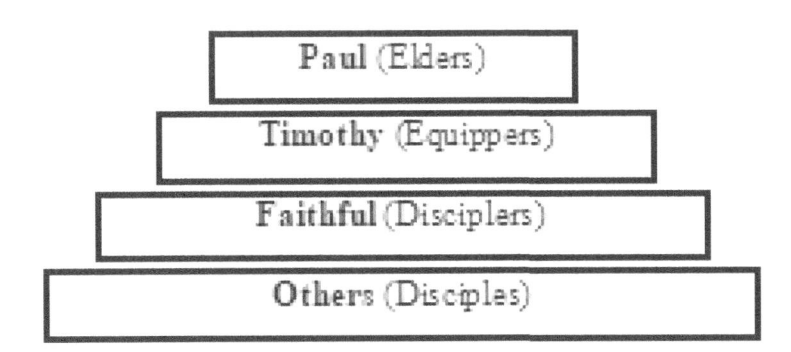

```
        Paul (Elders)
      Timothy (Equippers)
     Faithful (Disciplers)
      Others (Disciples)
```

Paul had invested years of ministry into the life of Timothy who was now the "senior pastor" (so to speak) of the church at Ephesus. Second Timothy is written near the end of Paul's life and is often referred to as one of the "Pastoral Epistles" because of its wealth of practical instruction to those in church leadership. What Paul lays out here is a clear schematic of church structure. The entry level for a disciple is the level of others. "Others" are those who desire someone to have a ministry in their lives. This is where the largest number of church members are. It is important to recognize that because of giftedness or faithfulness some will never move beyond this level.

What separates the next level, the faithful, is a) that they are faithful, and/or b) that they are "able to teach others." Some will not reach a level of teaching others because of unfaithfulness. However, others will

Philosophy of Discipleship (Continued)

not reach that level, though they are faithful, simply because of giftedness. They will be true disciples, exhibiting an abiding walk with Christ, a heart for the Word, effective prayer, and the fruit of Christian character as well as practical ministry, and they may even function as leaders at the deacon level, but their ministry will not primarily be in teaching others. Scripturally, the primary distinction between elders and deacons is that elders are "*able to teach*" (1 Tim.3:2). In 1 Peter 4:10-11 we see spiritual gifts divided into two categories: a) speaking gifts (this would include prophesy, teaching, leading, and exhortation), and b) serving gifts (this would include mercy, giving, and service). Speaking gifts dominate the higher levels of our pyramid.

The third level, Timothys, are those who function as equippers. Ephesians 4:11-12 indicates that God gave apostles, prophets, evangelists, and pastor/teachers "*…for the equipping of the saints for the work of service.*" Again, we see that giftedness is a primary consideration for who reaches this level of service. What separates a "Timothy" from a "faithful" is that a Timothy's focus is no longer simply ministering to people, but rather, ministering through people. Their job is to equip others for effective ministry.

In the fourth level are the "Pauls;" those who function as elders. "Pauls" are those with the giftedness, maturity, and ministry experience to be able to give vision and direction. These elders function as the generals, marshalling the troops to more effective service. A healthy, mature church will clearly exhibit all four of these levels of maturity and ministry function.

Putting the Pieces Together

In summary, the clear Biblical mandate is that disciple-making is to be placed at the heart of the local church. The central product of the church is to be disciples, those who exhibit an abiding walk with Christ, a heart for the Word, effective prayer, and the fruit of Christian character as well as practical ministry. Though the programs of a church may change, the product never does. We saw that a healthy, mature church will have four levels of maturity and ministry function. It is important to note that what defines a person's contribution to this process is not simply their maturity and giftedness. The state of the church also defines where a person is, as well as what direction they need to head. If the church is populated entirely by "Others" (disciples), then even a "Paul" (elder) would have to function as one of the "Faithful" until other disciplers were raised up. Once this had taken place, they could then begin to function as a "Timothy" (equipper) and focus on having a ministry through the disciplers God provides. As other equippers are raised up and trained, then and only then could a "Paul" truly function as an elder, keeping the vision of disciple-making at the heart of the church.

PHILOSOPHY OF DISCIPLESHIP (CONTINUED)

Notes:

Philosophy of Missions

© Copyright 1998, 2005 Eddie Rasnake
You may reproduce this chapter at no charge as long as proper credit is given and no changes are made to the document.

The term "missions" is most often applied to speak of a church's involvement in taking the gospel to the world. More specifically, it is usually addressing a church or denomination's involvement in other countries. It is right that churches and denominations have a vision beyond themselves. A church that sees not the world has ceased to fulfill Gods intent. The world God created is the object of His affection, and He is not willing that any should perish. The mission of Christ was to seek and to save the lost. Therefore, the mission of the church, the body of Christ, must be to seek and to save the lost. There are many crucial Biblical perspectives that come into play when we look at missions.

Balancing the Tension of Biblical Truths

As with every area of Biblical philosophy, right practice in missions must be preceded by right philosophy. A correct view of missions requires that we first identify a balanced view of what the Scriptures teach about missions, and then use that view to define in practical terms the right and wrong approaches to missions.

BIBLICAL REALITY #1: MISSIONS IS ABOUT A TASK, NOT JUST A TRIP

There is a tendency to view missions as something that happens when we leave our country and travel to another. But the true focus of missions is on "what," not "where." It is a healthy church who recognizes that the mission field begins outside her walls instead of across the globe. In fact, I know a church that has posted over each exit door a sign which reads "You are now entering the Mission field."

  Read Mark 16:15 and make note of what Christ instructed to His disciples after the resurrection.

  Looking at Matthew 28:18-20 verse by verse, write your observations on Christ's commission to His followers.

- 28:18

- 28:19

- 28:20

Jesus said that one of the consequences of being under the influence of the Holy Spirit is that we would be "witnesses." God has called the church to proclaim Him. Mark 16:15 makes it clear that we have a responsibility to go to the world and take the gospel to "*all creation.*" But this task is not only concerned with evangelism. In Matthew 28 we see that we are called to "*make disciples,*" not merely to recruit converts. This call to make disciples of all the nations is not a suggestion, but a command. Because "*all authority in heaven and on earth*" has been given to Christ, He has absolute right to command us, and He has. Further, not only have we been commanded, but we have also been commissioned. The apostle Paul calls us "*ambassadors for Christ,*" assigned the ministry of reconciliation and equipped with its message (see 1 Corinthians 5). These dual tasks of evangelism and discipleship are like the pedals on a bicycle. Though one is sometimes pushed harder than the other, our feet never leave either one. These make up the mission of the church.

Philosophy of Missions (Continued)

Biblical Reality #2: Missions is not simply something that happens elsewhere

Which would most people identify as a more worthy ministry to support with their efforts and finances—building an orphanage on the other side of the world or sharing the gospel on the other side of town?

📖 Read Acts 1:8 and make observations on the geographical implications of what Christ says, especially as it relates to answering the question above.

To accomplish its mission, the early church did not start with a trip to the far reaches of the planet. They began in Jerusalem—their own hometown. As they made disciples there, their manpower was reproduced. This insured that they not only could continue the work in Jerusalem, but also expand it into Judea and Samaria. By succeeding there as well, they continued their expansion to the uttermost parts of the world. It is important to distinguish that the church was to add these locations to their focus, NOT switch their focus to the new places. When we think of "gospel need" we tend to do so emotionally more than rationally. We think the impoverished need Christ more than the wealthy, and that a mission to a third world country is somehow more spiritual. It may surprise you to know that there are far more missionaries per capita in Papua New Guinea than in the city of Boston.

Biblical Reality #3: Every person is sinful and deserving of God's wrath

Scriptures clearly teach that every person is fallen, and apart from Christ, hopelessly lost and in need of redemption. Sin does not originate with a wrong choice. Sinful choices are the inevitable consequence of a fallen nature. The holiness of God requires separation from sin, so as a result of one's sinful nature and sinful choices he or she is separated from God. This reality is rooted in the holiness and purity of God Himself.

📖 Look at Romans 3:23 and write what it teaches about human sin.

📖 Now look at Romans 6:23 and identify the consequences of human sin.

Biblical Reality #4: God loves every person

Another Biblical perspective we must maintain as we look at a philosophy of missions is that redemption is as consistent with the character of God as is judgment. While it is the holiness of God that requires sin to be judged, it is the love of God, equally His nature, which moves Him to provide each of us the way to be redeemed. These attributes of God are not at war with each other but are both completely consistent with who God is.

📖 Read 2 Peter 3:9 and make note of God's attitude toward the people He created.

📖 John 3:16 is almost so familiar as to make it difficult to really appreciate its message. Look at it in light of the subject of God's love and write your observations here.

SERVANT APPROACH LEADERSHIP TRAINING: Building Biblical Philosophy   (revised 2/20/223)

PHILOSOPHY OF MISSIONS (CONTINUED)

BIBLICAL REALITY #5: GOD DOES NOT NEED OUR HELP

An additional Biblical reality, and perhaps the easiest to lose sight of as we look at the church's role in missions, is that God is self-sufficient. He does not need our help. He is fully capable of reaching fallen people with the reality of sin, righteousness, and judgment and with the message of redemption, and He needs no help whatsoever. In addition, the completion of the task of world evangelization is not in doubt. God, in His providence and power, has guaranteed that every ear will hear and that the heathen who rejects Him will be without excuse. Before a word slips from the lips of the gospel-bearer, God has already spoken. Through creation around them and conscience inside them each person has clearly seen God before a word is said (Romans 1 & 2) and he or she is already accountable for this knowledge. Further, because God is a just God, He will not withhold redemption and the redemption message from the humble and penitent if the assigned gospel-bearer fails to fulfill their task.

Look at each of the verses listed below and summarize their message about God's character.

- Jeremiah 32:17,27
- Matthew 19:26
- Luke 3:8
- Romans 1:18-20
- Romans 2:14-15
- Revelation 14:6-7

It is on the basis of these realities that any philosophy of missions must be founded. All deficiencies, deviations, and unbiblical excesses in world evangelization can be traced to an inadequate understanding of and submission to these realities. In a very real sense, these define the "what" of world evangelization. It should be noted that there are many other verses which could be added to this list.

The Consequences of Misbelief on World Evangelization

A wrong presupposition will always lead to a wrong conclusion, no matter how sound the logic is. It is worthwhile to consider the consequences of misbelief in each of these areas on the task of world evangelization. This consideration will not, of course, be exhaustive, but will give us a place to start. First, let us consider some of the results of misbelief of Biblical reality #1. What practical consequence would you expect when Missions is defined as a trip instead of a task?

It is important not only to see that you don't have to take a trip to involve yourself in missions, but it is also important to recognize that we can take a trip and perform a charitable service without embracing the mission of God. Digging a well for a villager in Africa accomplishes nothing of eternal consequence except that it is combined with the water which causes one to never thirst again. Since God has given to us the ministry of reconciliation, we have a responsibility to seek His face in a heart of surrender. We will never capture God's dream for our lives as individuals apart from also grasping His heart for His world.

PHILOSOPHY OF MISSIONS (CONTINUED)

We must *"beseech the Lord of the harvest to send out workers,"* and we must be willing to be an answer to that prayer.

What potential consequences do you see flowing out of wrongly defining Missions by geography?

In the verses we considered previously both Mark and Matthew indicated that the whole world is the target of our mission. Holding this truth by itself, however, has produced some erroneous values in the church. Most view missions as what happens in other countries, yet this is more a tradition than a truth. Our mission revolves around what we do, not where we do it. Since the whole world is the focus of the Great Commission, our target includes across the street as well as around the world. We cannot identify one as more important than the other. Though a church does well to become involved in reaching other countries, its members will never be as effective in reaching another culture as they will their own. Further, if a person is not effectively involved in reaching out in their own culture, a plane ride won't suddenly change things. As I mentioned before, if the early church ceased the work in Jerusalem because of prioritizing the world, their hometown would eventually cease to be a sender of missionaries and would instead become a mission field. This is not merely theory or hyperbole. It is a proven reality. At the turn of the 20th Century, Great Britain produced most of the planet's missionaries. At the beginning of the 21st Century, there are more practicing Muslims in Great Britain than there are practicing Christians. This is because they forgot about Jerusalem on their way to the uttermost parts. Missions may be a program, but our mission is the task of making disciples of all nations, identifying them with Christ and His family and teaching them to obey the commands of the Lord. Perhaps we ought to change the title of our budgets and programs from "missions" to "mission."

What do you think will result from not believing people are sinful and headed for judgment?

If the church does not really believe in human sinfulness and the coming judgment of God, then the task of world evangelization will become redefined. No longer will the spiritual state of people's souls be the primary focus, but instead, the church's attention will shift to temporal concerns. The church will simply become one more in a long line of humanitarian organizations. While the church should respond to the temporal needs of the world with the compassion of God, meeting temporal needs only will never address the real human problem. It will instead, enslave the church to the endless task of mopping up the symptoms of sin. A second danger of misbelief concerning human sinfulness is that of abandoning the task as altogether unnecessary.

What do you think will result from not believing in God's love and redemptive heart?

PHILOSOPHY OF MISSIONS (CONTINUED)

Misbelief in this Biblical reality can lead to equally serious consequences. If the church loses sight of the redemptive heart of God, the sinner will be viewed through the eyes of the Pharisee. The church will begin to become self-righteous and prideful and will cease to become the agent of love God created it to be. Sinners will be castigated for their immorality instead of lovingly presented with the solution to it. Instead of embracing the world as needy of Christ, the church will retreat from sinners and arrogantly judge them worthy of wrath.

What would you expect to result from not believing God's ability to accomplish the task of world evangelization apart from us?

This Biblical reality is especially prone to misbelief and the result to the church is an abandonment of the Christ life. Too many missionary appeals are based on a deficient view of God. Often, we are guilty of presenting world evangelization as our task instead of God's. We forget that it is HIS harvest and His job to send out workers into that harvest. An effective speaker can easily excite pity in his hearers, not only for the helpless heathen but also for the God who has tried so hard and so long to save them and has failed for lack of help. It is time for the church to conclude with Job: "*I know that You can do all things, and that no purpose of Yours can be thwarted.*" Otherwise, people will begin to respond to missionary appeal through the impotent efforts of the flesh. A. W. Tozer states, "I fear that thousands of younger persons enter Christian service from no higher motive than to help deliver God from the embarrassing situation His love has gotten Him into and His limited abilities seem unable to get Him out of. Add to this a certain degree of commendable idealism and a fair amount of compassion for the underprivileged and you have the true drive behind much Christian activity today." Instead of such erroneous thinking, we must recognize with Esther that if we remain silent, "*relief and deliverance will arise . . . from another place,*" (Esther 4:14) and it is we, not the cause, who will be the loser. If God truly is self-sufficient, then we must assume that the need for world evangelization is ours, not His. It is through participating in what God is doing that the church begins to value the things of God. It is through giving to the work of the Lord that heaven begins to become our treasure and the place where our heart is. It is not God who needs us, but we who need to be involved in what God is doing.

Understanding the self-sufficiency of God does not paralyze Christian labor—it energizes it. This truth, while being a necessary rebuke to human self-dependence, will (when seen scripturally) lift from us the exhausting weight of trying to figure out how to win the world for God, and in its place, we will find ourselves carrying the easy yoke of the Lord, being led by Him in Christ-initiated, Spirit-empowered labor to the honor and glory of God.

A Working Philosophy of Missions

The scope of world evangelization is defined by God in Acts 1:8, where Jesus proclaims to His disciples, "*... and you shall be My witnesses both in Jerusalem, and in all Judea and Samaria, and even to the remotest part of the earth.*" This scope reflects the heart of God, in that He is "*not wishing for any to perish but for all to come to repentance.*" The church's ability to fulfill this call "*to the remotest part of the earth*" is, according to Jesus, contingent on two factors: receiving "*power*," and "*the Holy Spirit coming upon you.*" Both of these prerequisites have God as their source and work to define who does what. It is the indwelling and filling of the Holy Spirit that defines the parameters of each believer's role in world evangelization. This is done through the work of God in the heart and life as He has gifted, called, and burdened each of us. This tells the "where" of world evangelization to each individual. We

PHILOSOPHY OF MISSIONS (CONTINUED)

must be careful of unbiblical distinctions. The called person overseas is no more or less important to the work of God than here. We can trust that if we put the emphasis on the call of God, He will call where the need is, for it is His harvest.

The initiative of world evangelization is God's, not ours. This is an essential reality to understand. In Matthew 9:38 Jesus makes it clear that it is *"the Lord of the harvest"* who sends out *"workers into His harvest."* If our focus is the need of the world instead of the Lord of the harvest, our response will be wrong, however well intentioned. This makes the call of God the crucial imperative. It tells the "who" of world evangelization. God's call always comes with His provision of giftedness and resources.

The resourcing of world evangelization is the responsibility of God and the privilege of each of us. These two realities are not at odds with each other. The privilege of participation in missions reflects no need on the part of God, but rather, His gracious intent to let us participate in what He is doing. Whenever we look at ministry in any form we must remember: "Where God guides, God provides." This tells the "how" of world evangelization. If any ministry venture lacks resources, then either we are not looking to God for how he wants to provide those resources, or we are not where He has guided. This does not negate the element of faith, for God does not always provide when and how we expect or desire.

We see from these three considerations that the "where," the "who," and the "how" of missions are all in the hands of God, not us.

How Does a Church Select Missionary Candidates?

A final consideration is the question of how a church should decide who to support and how much. At the risk of sounding simplistic, the bottom line is they must hear from God. Supporting a missionary is as important an involvement in the harvest as going and requires as much a call. We must beseech the Lord of the harvest for wisdom. Logic would tell us that we cannot support everyone who asks, so what criteria do we use to make such a decision? First, we should only support those who have a clearly identifiable call and have been adequately equipped to fulfill it. Second, our criteria for the field should be no different than our criteria at home. If we would not hire a person to serve at our church, then we should not be supporting them to go somewhere else. The mission field deserves no less than our best. This means that a missionary candidate must meet the same Scriptural requirements as a pastor. Remember, the first missionaries (Barnabas and Paul) were pastors sent out by their church. Along with this, we should hold our supported missionaries to the same doctrinal standards as our pastors and teachers. We have no business supporting someone to teach on the mission field what we would not allow in our pulpit. These standards if dutifully followed would provide a more concrete basis for evaluation of support requests and would make it easier to be good stewards with our missions giving.

How Does a Church Prioritize its Missions Spending?

A final area a church must consider is how to take the resources allocated to the area of missions and use them in a way that reflects their values and has the greatest impact. Research into the evolution of missions giving of churches where missions was a great priority reveals some interesting patterns. There is a tendency toward some common strengths as well as some common mistakes. Churches with a strong missions heart reflect this value in their overall budget. Missions spending is significant, and sometimes is extreme. But the priorities of that spending tend to change as the ministry matures. To fully appreciate the decision-making dilemmas a church must face in this area, answer the questions below.

In a general sense, to what percentage of an individual missionary's support do you believe a local church should commit?

SERVANT APPROACH LEADERSHIP TRAINING: Building Biblical Philosophy   (revised 2/20/223)

Philosophy of Missions (Continued)

How should the decision to support or the amount of support be affected by…

♦ Whether the missionary was raised up from that church, joined that church after already being in ministry, or simply came to the church for support?

♦ The missionary being an "expatriate" (foreign to their field) verses "indigenous" (national worker)?

♦ What the missionary does verses where it is done?

♦ Whether it is evangelistic ministry, edifying ministry, equipping ministry or benevolent?

♦ Whether the ministry is stateside or overseas?

♦ What country or region of the world the missionary is to serve in?

♦ Under what circumstances should a missionary's support be increased?

♦ Under what circumstances should a missionary's support be decreased or discontinued?

Most new churches or churches with a new emphasis in missions determine to give larger amounts to each missionary. The rationale is that by making a significant, rather than token commitment, they can make a bigger difference in those ministries they support. They can lessen the time a missionary spends on initial support raising, as well as on reporting during a furlough. Churches can and should give larger amounts than individuals. There is however one significant problem with this approach. It doesn't acknowledge the fundamental reality that whether their gifts are large or small, sooner or later the budget will be used up. Unless the church has first defined is parameters and priorities, this approach rewards those who enter the system early and punishes those who arrive when the funds are gone, with little regard for strategic giving. What most churches learn later in the process is that they should have defined their priorities and standards up front and should have allocated conservatively. It is always easier to increase later than decrease. In the process of wrestling with too many opportunities (and as soon as word gets out in the missions community there will be plenty), values emerge and are defined. Priorities become established. Standards are inevitably raised. But really, all of that should have been tackled up front. The investment opportunities are too great to give to everyone who comes to your door.

What values should guide who a church supports and how much? While a church should be open to supporting strangers, its first priority is to those raised up from within. If a home church does not get behind its own missionary, it sends a negative message. Many mission ministries have also learned the value of supporting national workers. In many countries, whether because there are few Christians or because of economic conditions, it is only through foreign support that a Christian worker is able to devote themselves full-time to the ministry. Often the cost of such support is only a fraction of what it would be to

PHILOSOPHY OF MISSIONS (CONTINUED)

send a missionary there from the states—especially when factoring in learning the language and culture. The downside of such giving though is that such issues as communication and accountability often are difficult. Also, a rookie national worker is not more effective than a veteran missionary just because he is cheaper. Another consideration that few missions committees think about up front is the distinction between those who offer direct ministry in evangelism and discipleship verses indirect ministry such as construction or medical care. Though both are valid, they shouldn't be approached as being the same priority. Support decisions should be driven by a rational approach rather than an emotional one. Raising money for orphanages is easier than for pastoral training because a picture of a homeless child tugs harder at the heart than one of a studying pastor. Results reported from an evangelistic crusade sound more impressive that results from a discipleship emphasis because they are more immediate. But without discipleship, those results will disappear as fast as they appeared. A life-changing discipleship process is harder to write about in a newsletter than a conversion. This is why giving must be guided by the mind as well as the heart.

Ask any missionary who has done both and they will tell you that it is far easier to raise money to go overseas than to minister in the States. I have a friend who lost over 50% of his support when his Mission Board called him home from Africa to serve in a more strategic leadership role at their headquarters in the US. This is because most of us wrongly value geography over strategy and calling. Many churches want to have different standards for missionaries to "unreached" peoples. There is nothing wrong with valuing those areas with fewer Christians. We must remember though that the harvest belongs to God, and it is He who determines which fields are ready to harvest. We need to keep our eyes on God, for need does not equal call. A church that commits to mission support should count the cost. Taking on their first missionary at 50% of their support will likely bring challenges down the road in either the ability to support others or to maintain that commitment or both. While churches who have overcommitted sometimes have to drop to a lower level of support, this is always painful for everyone involved and can negatively affect ministry. Better to have counted the cost up front than to have to make cuts for not having done so. A church needs a sense of calling to a particular ministry, but that calling may not be permanent. If changes need to occur, they should be communicated as far in advance as possible, with a view to when the missionary will be able to replace the lost support. What is the bottom line? A church needs to define its mission philosophy, standards and priorities <u>before</u> committing to support, and it needs to continually evaluate that support commitment based on the following factors:

- Effectiveness. This is not based on visible results or numbers alone. In some cases, the missionary "effort" is more important than the numbers alone.
- Where God is working. When the Lord is moving in a particular area or opens wide the door, that should be prioritized (e.g. when the Iron Curtain fell, the Soviet region opened for the gospel. In many of those countries, that openness was short-lived).
- Completion of the task. When a missionary completes the task they were called to do, it is often essential to the growth of the body of Christ in that country for them to not stay too long. Otherwise, they become a hindrance to the development of national leaders. In the long run, national workers must take the lead and foreign missionaries <u>must</u> be working themselves out of a job. Jesus didn't stick around forever.
- Partnership—The ability of the church to have a continuing relationship with the work. If a church supports too many missionaries in too many different directions, their connection to the world is actually lessened. Fewer missionaries in specifically targeted areas will build a relationship between the body and the missionary that will lead to a more prayer, more special giving, more encouragement...a more committed partnership.

SESSION 5: HOMEWORK SUMMARY

Due Date: _____

Review of homework assignments:

Philosophy of Church

© Copyright 2022 Eddie Rasnake
You may reproduce this chapter at no charge as long as proper credit is given and no changes are made to the document.

What is the church? Most of us are familiar with "churches." In the city where I currently reside, there are hundreds of them in every shape, size, and denomination. But what is THE Church? It isn't a term you find in the Old Testament, although a case can be made that the idea is there. So, what is it? What defines it? Is it required to have gothic spires, or a steeple adorned with a cross? Is it a church if it doesn't have a building, or if it meets in a home? When establishing a philosophy of church, we must recognize that although there are ample Scriptures we can reference, for most of us our view of the church, both local and universal, is shaped as much or more by culture and experience as it is by the Bible. The only cure for that is to examine what God has to say about His church.

What is the Church?

📖 The first mention in the Bible of the term "church" is Matthew 16:18. Read the verse in its context (16:13-18) and record what you learn.

In Matthew 16 Jesus is having a conversation with His disciples that begins with a question: "Who do people say that the Son of Man is?" The disciples would have understood the term as a reference to the Messiah. After differing views are mentioned, He personalizes the question, and asks "*But who do you say that I am?*" Simon Peter gets it right for once. "*You are the Christ (Messiah), the Son of the living God.*" In fairness, Peter can't really take credit for the win, for Jesus makes it clear that this was not arrived at by reason, but rather, through revelation. Jesus goes on to make a definitive statement about the church: "…upon this rock I will build My church; and the gates of Hades will not overpower it." With this statement, the church era begins. Notice first that Christ makes it clear that THE church belongs to Him and is built by Him. He is speaking of the church universal, and that would include every local church. Second, the foundation upon which the church is built is the revelation that Jesus is the Messiah and the Son of the living God. He is not merely a good moral teacher or promoter of ethics and philosophy. The reference to the gates of Hades makes it clear that the church will face opposition, but the promise of Christ is that His church will prevail.

The term translated "church" in Matthew 16 and elsewhere in the New Testament is *ekklesia* and is not a strictly religious term. It simply means "the assembly" or "the gathering." It is used in Acts 19:32 and 38-39 in a secular sense: "*So then, some were shouting one thing and some another, for the assembly was in confusion and the majority did not know for what reason they had come together…*"; "*So then, if Demetrius and the craftsmen who are with him have a complaint against any man, the courts are in session and proconsuls are available; let them bring charges against one another. "But if you want anything beyond this, it shall be settled in the lawful assembly.*" The cultural meaning was a particular, intentional gathering of people who assembled for a specific purpose. By both its Biblical and cultural usage it is clear that it is more than simply a generic gathering in someone's home of people who happen to be Christians. As the church adopted this terminology from Christ to refer to the weekly meeting of believers to worship God, it appears to have faded from secular use.

PHILOSOPHY OF CHURCH (CONTINUED)

Although "church" is not mentioned in the Old Testament, the idea of an intentional assembly of God's people can be found there. In Acts 7:38 Stephen refers to the gathering or "congregation" of Israel at Mount Sinai (recorded in Exodus 19:1-6) as an *ekklesia*. We often wrongly use the term "church" to refer to a building where Christians gather, but this is Biblically incorrect. God's people don't enter a church; the church (God's people) sometimes enter a building. Another cultural (but unbiblical) usage of "church" is to refer to a denomination – such as the United Church of Christ, or the Presbyterian Church in America (PCA) or the Church of England. When the hierarchy of these denominations speak on behalf of their respective organizations, they do not represent all the Christians in America or England or wherever, or even all the individual churches in those areas.

📖 Look at the verses below and identify how they describe Christ's church.

1 Corinthians 1:2

Hebrews 12:23

1 Timothy 3:4-5

1 Timothy 3:15

Revelation 19:7-8; 21:1-2

We may use terminology such as "the Corinthian Church" but Paul is careful not to reference them in such an imprecise fashion. He speaks of this local gathering of believers as the "church of God in Corinth." The church universal meets in different locations, but from God's perspective there is only one church – not a myriad of independent churches. When one looks at the religious landscape in America and around the world, it is clear that not all who attend a given church or even all who join it formally are truly Christians. In Hebrews 12 the writer clarifies that the church is those who are "enrolled" (literally "written down") in heaven. When Paul gives criteria for church leadership, he speaks of the "household of God." What he is saying is that the church is a family. That is why Scripture refers to other believers as our "brothers and sisters." At the end of 1 Timothy 3 we see this "household" word again referring to the church and are told it is the "pillar and support" of the truth. In Revelation we find a final metaphor for the church: the bride of Christ.

Why Do We Need Church?

Is it acceptable to be a follower of Jesus without being part of a local church? In many parts of the world, church attendance is declining. Part of the reason for the statistical drop is that with the plethora of Christian materials and media available, some people who identify as followers of Jesus don't feel the need for a local gathering with other believers. Often, they feel they can find better, more engaging preaching and worship online than on site. Another, less obvious reason for declining weekly church attendance is that even among those who consider themselves "regular" attenders of a local gathering,

PHILOSOPHY OF CHURCH (CONTINUED)

faithfulness is no longer defined by showing up several times a week. In fact, because of travel or sports or work or other competing events, the level of engagement by those "regulars" is around 1.9 visits per month. That means that a church that averages 500 in weekly attendance may have 1,000 members who consider themselves regulars. Of course, when not there in person they can often join virtually through live-streaming or catch a video or audio of at least part of the service later online or even on our phones. The Covid-19 pandemic has made such options more readily available and more "normal." Does it really matter all that much if we show up on a given Sunday? You may be uncomfortable making such a statement, but a close examination of your behavior may make a statement of a different kind. I don't say that to guilt you into attendance, but rather as a segue to attempting to answer such questions from Scripture. Let me say up front that I believe whether we are with God's people on a given Sunday actually matters a lot more than we realize.

📖 Reflect on the verses that follow and make note of what you learn about why it matters for us to be physically present at the *ekklesia*.

Galatians 3:26-28

Romans 12:5

Acts 2:42-47

1 Corinthians 12:27

One fundamental perspective the Bible calls us to adopt is to recognize that one can't come to Christ without coming to His people. In fact, our relationship with Christ shapes our relationship with one another. God calls us to a unity with our fellow Christians. Paul goes so far as to say in Romans 12:5 "*...so we, who are many, are one body in Christ, and individually members one of another.*" To attempt to live the Christian life on our own is a spiritual schizophrenia – separating ourselves from ourselves. A body part separated from the body cannot function as it was intended to operate. There are 59 "one another" commands in Scripture. We are commanded by Christ to love one another, to pray for one another, to minister to one another, to encourage one another, and to forgive one another just to name a few. These commands are not framed as suggestions, and the vast majority of them cannot be fulfilled without being with one another.

In Acts 2 we are given a glimpse of the priorities and practices of the early church. They were continually devoting themselves to four priorities: the apostles' teaching (the verbal form of what would become the New Testament) and to fellowship, to the breaking of bread, and to prayer. Maybe we can argue that we can get teaching and spiritual food even if we don't attend on a given Sunday. It is much harder to satisfy the call to koinonia in abstentia. Likewise, the breaking of bread (communion) is a sacrament which requires local participation. While we can pray even if we aren't present, it is unlikely we will be as aware

PHILOSOPHY OF CHURCH (CONTINUED)

of what to pray for if we don't attend, and we might miss out on the prompting to do so without seeing God's people. Clearly, these verses assume participation and presence. In 1 Corinthians 12:27 we are reminded that we are "Christ's body." We are His hands, His feet, and His heart on planet earth. The church cannot be all it is intended to be without our presence.

📖   What additional truths do you find in the following passages that speak to the question "does it really matter if we show up".

Matthew 25:40

1 Corinthians 12:7

1 Peter 4:10-11

Ephesians 4:15-16

Luke 22:25-27

Jesus indicated that whatever we have done to the least of His brethren, we have done to Him. If we neglect being with and ministering to the people of God, do we not neglect Him? Clearly, we have all been endowed with certain spiritual gifts. Paul tells the Corinthians that these endowments are not for our own selfish benefit, but for the "common good." Peter expresses it this way: "don't let your spiritual gifts be unemployed! Put them to work serving others!" To the Ephesian believers Paul makes it clear that the body of Christ is built and defined and held together "*by what every joint supplies, according to the proper working of each individual part.*" The church will not and cannot be all it is intended to be without our presence. The modern church is being undermined by believers with a consumer mindset who look to be served instead of to serve. If our calling is to be like Christ, remember what He said, "*I am among you as the one who serves.*"

What do we miss out on if we do not participate in the local church?

While I would be the last one to advocate approaching church with a consumer mindset, I would be remiss if I neglected to mention that in addition to missing out on opportunities to serve if we neglect involvement with God's people, we also miss out on important things we are intended to receive as well.

📖   Write your observations on the following verses and what they teach about what the body of Christ adds to our lives.

Hebrews 3:13

Hebrews 10:24-25

Philosophy of Church (Continued)

John 13:35

Galatians 6:1-2, 6

The writer of Hebrews reminds us, *"But encourage one another day after day, as long as it is still called 'Today,' so that none of you will be hardened by the deceitfulness of sin."* When we neglect identifying with a local gathering of believers and fail to worship with them regularly, we rob ourselves of much needed encouragement, and put ourselves at risk of being hardened by sin's deceitfulness. We are commanded to assemble with one another. I don't see any exceptions or exemption clauses to let us off the hook here. In fact, Hebrews 10 makes it clear that the closer we get to Christ's return, the greater the need is to be with God's people. If we neglect the assembly, not only do we miss out on being able to stimulate others to love and good deeds, we rob ourselves of that much needed stimulation from others. We are called and commanded to love one another. Do we really think we can do that from a distance? Paul exhorts us in Galatians 6: *"Brethren, even if anyone is caught in any trespass, you who are spiritual, restore such a one in a spirit of gentleness; each one looking to yourself, so that you too will not be tempted. Bear one another's burdens, and thereby fulfill the law of Christ."* When we neglect assembling with the family of God, we lose out on much needed accountability. We rob ourselves of a helping hand when we stumble. We must bear our burdens alone. Verse 6 adds the reminder that to be able to be taught and to have the opportunity to bless those teachers in return by sharing with them, we have to be present.

Bill Bright, the founder of Campus Crusade for Christ (Cru), employed the following graphic analogy in his evangelistic booklet called "The Four Spiritual Laws": several logs burn brightly together, but place one by itself on the hearth and the fire quickly goes out. It is difficult to maintain our spiritual fervency without the encouragement, challenge, and example of other Christians. Christianity is not a solo sport. From the very beginning, God set the course. In the perfection of the garden of Eden, before sin had left its stain, God created piece after piece of His planned design, and each piece was good. Yet in that perfection there was one thing that was not good: *"It is not good for man to be alone"* (Genesis 2:18).

What does a good church member look like?

We've seen in the Scriptures the clear and compelling case for our need to be part of the church. So, what does faithfulness to that calling look like? Clearly, it is not enough simply to have a membership card at First Baptist of Anywhereville that we never use. After devoting the entire eleventh chapter to listing a "hall of fame" of the great saints of the Old Testament era, the writer of Hebrews begins chapter 12 with these words: *"Therefore, since we have so great a cloud of witnesses surrounding us...let us run with endurance the race that is set before us."* He is using the idea of a stadium as an illustration, and in this metaphor, the saints who have finished their race are in the stands cheering us on as we run. The point is clear. If we are still alive, we are to be on the field; not sitting in the stands as a spectator.

I'd like to close with some simple suggestions from the Scriptures of what it looks like to be a faithful participant in Christ's bride, the church. A member of the body of Christ is called to…

- **Attend regularly** (Hebrews 10:24). In other words, unless I am providentially hindered, it shouldn't ever be a question of whether I will show up, regardless of if I feel like going or not. It isn't just about me and my needs and wants.

Philosophy of Church (Continued)

- **Be involved** (Ephesians 4:15-16). We should be actively involved, not keeping our distance as a spectator. It is our church, and we should a) know what is going on, and b) have a stake in where it is heading.
- **Pray** (James 5:16). God has designed our world in such a way that we can actually make a difference not only by our actions, but also by our asking.
- **Serve** (1 Peter 4:10). The credit for a great church lies not simply in those up front, but in "the proper working of each individual part." It is easy to criticize, but it is more honorable to do something about the needs we want to criticize.
- **Give** (Proverbs 3:9-10). Giving financially to your church is a way of directing your heart there, for where our treasure is, there will our heart be. The church always has needs, but our need to be giving is always the greatest one.
- **Submit** (Hebrews 13:17). Obviously, we do not submit to decisions that are sinful and violate Scripture. However, the person who hops from church to church because of some minor point of disagreement never learns the important lesson of submitting to leaders. Instead, they find each move easier to make, and by their example they teach their children not to submit to spiritual authority.

PHILOSOPHY OF CHURCH (CONTINUED)

Notes:

PHILOSOPHY OF RESTORATION

© Copyright 1998 Eddie Rasnake Associate Pastor of Discipleship and
Steve McCary, Associate Pastor of Counseling, Woodland Park Baptist Church

You may reproduce this chapter at no charge as long as proper credit is given and no changes are made to the document.

When looking at this area of sin and restoration, the pivotal issue everything else revolves around is the responsibility of the church to speak the Word of God to its members (Hebrews 13:7) and to keep watch over their souls (Hebrews 13:17). This same passage tells us that it is the church leadership who will *"give an account"* to God for such watch care. Since *"a little leaven leavens the whole lump of dough"* (1 Corinthians 5:6) and rebellion in the body that is not addressed affects the whole body. Everyone who sees rebellion in the body that the leadership is unwilling to address is encouraged to take their own sin less seriously. Sin must be dealt with and this process is often referred to as "church discipline." But discipline is only one facet of the restoration process, and perhaps even more significant, the discipline component exists not as an end in itself, but to facilitate the overarching objective which is restoration. Therefore, we refer to this process as the "Ministry of Restoration."

  Read 1 Corinthians 5:1 through 6:11 and 2 Corinthians 2:6-11. Scholars believe that Paul is referring to the same person in both accounts. Even if the two accounts are unrelated, it does give us a vivid picture of church discipline and restoration in the early church. Answer the following questions based on your observations:

- For what did Paul want to discipline this person?

- What form did Paul expect the discipline to take?

- What attitude did Paul expect the church to take in response to this person's sin?

- What is Paul's goal in disciplining this person?

- Who is responsible for the discipline?

- How do the verses in 1 Corinthian 6:1-11 relate to this person's sin?

- When a person responds appropriately to church discipline, what is to be the church's response?

- What are the consequences of a church only punishing a fallen brother or sister and refusing to accept them back after a true repentance?

PHILOSOPHY OF RESTORATION (CONTINUED)

Dealing With Sin in the Body

The *place* of discipline and restoration according to Matthew 18 is "the church." There is no higher court to appeal to, and no legal loopholes to sidestep through. If, after Biblical confrontation, a sinning brother or sister refuses to repent then their rebellion is to be told to the church (Matthew 18:17) so that they can participate in the process by also calling them to repentance, and by breaking fellowship if necessary. A rebellious, unrepentant brother or sister is to be treated as a gentile or a tax-gatherer was by first century Jews. The discipline component is not merely a "wrist-slap" by the elders behind closed doors.

The *purpose* of discipline is <u>not</u> punishment, but restoration. Discipline does not exist for its own sake, but as a tool of the church to be handled with love and discernment for the purpose of bringing about the restoration of a sinning member. This is accomplished by faithfully holding in place the consequences of sin so they may act. Sin breaks spiritual fellowship and unity because the one sinning is no longer in the Spirit and able to relate spirit to spirit (Ephesians 4:13) with a surrendered believer. If this broken fellowship is not also maintained physically, then the relationship is redefined, and the consequences of the sin are not held in place. The sinner is allowed to hold on to their sin while their relationships, though stained, remain intact. This is not God's way. Breaking fellowship, an act the whole body participates in, is God's way of isolating the sinner with their sin and helping them see more quickly how distasteful it really is. The motive behind this is so he or she will come to their senses like the prodigal son, they will remember how much better it was before, and they will return in repentance. The motive can never be vengeance, for that belongs to God alone.

 📖 The Greek word used for "restore" is *katartizo* (Strong's #2675). Record its definition:

 📖 Read 1 Corinthians 1:10 in both the NAS and KJV and find where *katartizo* is used. How does its usage in this passage relate to your definition above? How does it relate to the idea of restoration?

The *person* of discipline initially is the offended brother or sister (Matthew 18:15), not some committee of spiritual henchmen. Hopefully, in most cases, that is all that will be needed to correct the situation. It is the responsibility of every member in the body who is spiritual (Galatians 6:1) to address the sin they see. The purity of the body is every believer's concern. This is more than simply a prayer of wishful thinking. It often will require loving confrontation. This responsibility of the individual can be neither side-stepped nor delegated to another.

The *provocation* of discipline is, according to Matthew 18:15, *"if your brother sins"* (many manuscripts add *"against you"*). The types of sin are not listed. The reference is kept general because it doesn't really matter. All sin must be addressed. Of course, not all sin can or should be addressed by the elders. But if the body is working properly, most individuals will be dealing with their own sin, and from time to time it will become necessary for members to lovingly confront other members. Whenever any member of the body violates God's Word and is unrepentant it is sin and must be confronted. All sin is against another member either directly or indirectly. When someone punches me in the nose that is sinning against me directly and I must confront them in love, point out the sin, and call for repentance. However, all sins are

Philosophy of Restoration (Continued)

not that direct though. Any sin that brings reproach on the assembly of God's people stains us all. Their leaven affects the whole lump, even if it is directly against no one in the body. To ignore such sin because it has touched no one directly is to misunderstand the impact of sin. Sin in the camp affected more than just Achan. All sin disrupts the unity of the Spirit (Ephesians 4:3) and robs others of the ministry that member should have been able to offer.

The *prerequisites* of discipline are crucial to keep in focus. Before we can begin the process of going to our brother or sister, there are certain bases we must cover with ourselves. When you become aware of a sinning member, before the initial step of going to them in private, you must *"first take the log out of your own eye, and then you will see clearly to take the speck out of your brother's eye"* (Matthew 7:5). You must first examine yourself to see if there is sinful motivation for wanting to confront them. If your heart is right, then you will grieve over the need to confront, not rejoice over it. Also, the driving force behind your confrontation will be your brother or sister's good. The only reason to address the speck in another's eye is to benefit them, not yourself. The second issue to cover before beginning the process of discipline is an assessment of the root of the rebellion. The apostle Paul in 1 Thessalonians 5:14 identifies three different reasons why one might stray from the truth, each requiring a different response. He says, *"admonish the unruly, encourage the faint-hearted, help the weak."* Before confronting a sinning member, we must ask ourselves "are they unruly, are they faint-hearted, or are they weak?" The word "unruly" carries the idea of "out of line." If he or she has strayed from the prescribed life of Scripture, then such a one is to be continually admonished (present imperative). If he or she is faint-hearted (feeble-minded or weak headed, not knowing what to do), then they don't need admonishment, they need encouragement. If he or she is weak (without power, knowing what to do but unable to do it) then they need help (support). So how do you know which motivation is at the root of the problem? First, you must ask God for wisdom and insight. Second, you must err on the side of believing the best. You should approach them as if they are weak or faint-hearted, expecting to find a teachable, repentant heart. If one is unruly that will become evident by the response.

The *process* of discipline is clearly delineated in Matthew and the epistles.

Step 1

Once you have examined your own heart and taken it to the Lord, and once you have looked at what might be behind their error, I am then to *"go and show him his fault in private"* (literally "between you and him alone") (Matthew 18:15). Hopefully this is all that will be required. Jesus says, *"if he listens to you, you have won your brother."* But if they are unrepentant, I must move to Step 2. If you speak of the matter to anyone else before them or beside them then you have sinned.

Step 1 can take place in two forms:

A. The Sinning Believer is contacted by a Mature Believer strictly based on Matthew 18:15. If the Sinning Believer repents, Praise the Lord! No contact with church leadership is necessary.

B. If the local church leadership is approached by a brother or sister in the Lord for the purpose of informing of a Sinning Believer's behavior yet he or she has not personally gone to the Sinning Believer, it is the leadership's responsibility to do the following:

1. Lovingly instruct the approaching brother/sister concerning the Biblical restoration process. Have them read this publication as well as give specific assistance relative to the Prerequisites of Discipline and Step 1.

PHILOSOPHY OF RESTORATION (CONTINUED)

2. Since the approaching Mature Believer has brought the issue to the church, it now becomes the church leadership's responsibility to expect the Mature Believer to initiate the correct reconciliation encounter. If no contact is made by an agreed upon date, then the church leadership will contact the Mature Believer to determine if Step 1.B. has taken place. If the meeting has not taken place, the church leadership needs to determine why it has not and proceed to work toward Step 1 taking place by the Mature Believer (Serious reconsideration should be given to the validity of the Mature Believer's charge against the Sinning Believer and/or the Mature Believer's "maturity" based on their lack of follow through). It is possible, based on the seriousness of the charge and knowledge of the situation, that a now informed member of the church leadership carries out Step 1.

3. If, after the agreed upon date for Step 1 to have been completed has passed and church leadership repeatedly is unable to contact the Mature Believer, the church leadership will contact the Sinning Believer and say, "Brother/Sister, Mature Believer indicated to me that they were going to contact you on a very sensitive matter. Have they done so?" Clarify where needed and prayerfully proceed to setting up a meeting and proceed with Step 2.

STEP 2

Jesus says, *"but if he does not listen to you, take one or two more with you, so that by the mouth of two or three witnesses every fact may be confirmed"* (Matthew 18:16). Several issues must be clarified with this step. First, who qualifies as a witness? There is no indication that it is a matter for the elders at this point, but logic suggests that perhaps it would be wise to involve an elder or trusted representative of the elders.

The apostle Paul, in Galatians 6:1 indicates that the only criteria for witnesses are: *"you who are spiritual"* (any spirit-filled believer), and by inference, one who is able to do it *"in a spirit of gentleness,"* and one who is *"looking to yourself, so that you too will not be tempted."* James simply relegates the responsibility to *"brethren"* (James 5:19-20). A second issue to clarify is "to what are they witnesses?" Logically, it isn't a requirement that they be witnesses to the sin, but rather, they are there to witness to the fact of this brother's unwillingness to repent. The focus of discipline is no longer the symptom (immorality, stealing, etc.), but now the focus shifts to the root sin (rebellion, a lack of repentance).

📖 Read Deuteronomy 19:15-20 and answer the following questions based on your observations:
- Why is more than one witness needed prior to church discipline?

- To whom is an accusation made?

- Why is the response of those hearing an accusation confirmed by two or more witnesses?

- What is the purpose of discipline?

Here are the stages in properly handling Step 2:

A. Step 2 should include the offended Mature Believer involved in Step 1. In addition, one or two who are mature and knowledgeable enough of the situation so as to be effective, as the Lord leads, in the upcoming meeting.

PHILOSOPHY OF RESTORATION (CONTINUED)

B. If there is repentance, then counseling and appropriate accountability should be considered.

C. If repentance is not apparent, contact with church leadership must follow and a certified letter will be sent, indicating that a lack of response by a specified date (approximately 1 week), would then send this matter before the entire council of Elders. The 3 individuals who approached the Sinning Believer in Step 2 should sign this letter.

D. If repentance is not apparent following the certified letter by the Step 2 participants, the matter is brought before the Elders. They initiate another certified letter communicating that a lack of repentant response by specified date (i.e., the next Lord's Supper) will cause their name to be brought before the church body for the purpose of prayer and for the church to urge for repentance and reconciliation (Step 3). The church must be educated as to how to go about making any contact so as to prevent an immature and harsh contact that would draw the sinning member's attention away from his/her need to repent.

STEP 3

Jesus clarifies, *"If he refuses to listen to them* [the two or three witnesses], *tell it to the church"* (Matthew 18:17). The appropriate time for this would be the Lord's Supper, and the member should be notified in advance by registered mail. It is important to realize that this step is not for the purpose of public shame or excommunication. The focus is still the restoration of the sinning member. Jesus makes it clear by the next statement (*"and if he refuses to listen even to the church"*) that the aim is for the member to *"listen to the church."* There should be time given for the member to repent. It is important to identify that the central problem is not the initial sin, but the rebellion of unrepentance. It may be wise to give only limited information about what initiated the process of confrontation and to focus primarily on the believer's response to being confronted about his or her sin. If the efforts of the entire church are unable to secure the member's repentance within an appointed time period (presumably until the next Lord's Supper), then move to the fourth and final step.

A. If there is no response to the Elders (Step 2.D.) by the next scheduled Lord's Supper, then, in a non-dramatic yet serious manner, prior to the distribution of the elements of the covenant meal, the Sinning Believer's name is shared with the membership present by a representative of the Elders (other than the Senior Pastor). Enough of the details are shared to communicate the seriousness of the situation and to also curtail unnecessary private discussion. Of course, the purpose of this step is to enlist the prayer of the body as well as their involvement, as the Lord leads, in calling the individual to repentance. This statement should be prepared in advance and read to guard against misspeaking.

B. A certified letter by the Elders is sent to the Sinning Believer explaining what has happened and what will happen in Step 4, if repentance is not seen by the next scheduled Lord's Supper. Also included in this letter should be an explanation of what would happen if the Sinning Believer is repentant (counseling and accountability instituted and the congregation made aware of the joyful news).

STEP 4

Jesus tells us, *"...and if he refuses to listen even to the church, let him be to you as a Gentile and a tax-collector."* Essentially Jesus says, treat them as an unbeliever. We don't ignore them or ridicule them, but we also don't fellowship with them. All our contact with them is aimed at ministering and drawing them into fellowship with God. This same concept is reiterated by Paul in 2 Thessalonians 3:6 where we read: *"Now we command you, brethren, in the name of our Lord Jesus Christ, that you keep away from every*

Philosophy of Restoration (Continued)

brother who leads an unruly life and not according to the tradition which you received from us". His point is further clarified in 3:14-15 where we read: *"If anyone does not obey our instruction in this letter* [pre-canonized Scripture], *take special note of that person and do not associate with him, so that he will be put to shame. Yet do not regard him as an enemy, but admonish him as a brother."* Again, the member should be notified of this action by registered letter.

A. If there is no repentance, then, in similar manner as Step 3.A, share with congregation at the next scheduled Lord's Supper, the heart of the action taken in Step 4 (2 Thessalonians 3:6, 14-15).

B. If there is repentance, then, in similar manner as Step 3.A, share with congregation at the next scheduled Lord's supper with quiet & thankful rejoicing

KEY POINT:
Elder involvement should, by its very nature be a rarity since in essence it is a last resort

The Power

The *power* of discipline is illustrated in the verses of Matthew 18 that follow. There we are reminded that what we bind on earth (through rightly exercising church discipline) shall have been bound in heaven. We are not twisting the arm of God but aligning ourselves with it. When we do, and if the sinning member is still unrepentant, he or she is bound in their sins. God gives them over for the consequences of sin to do their dirty work. It is an interesting and unanswered question, but one must logically ask, "If we do not exercise church discipline biblically and fully, are we not impeding the working of God and the operation of the consequences of sin in the life of the unrepentant?" We may actually hinder the process of restoration. God is in the midst of the working of believers in church discipline if they are working toward His goal of restoration that is spelled out in the preceding verses (Matthew 18:12-14). Here Jesus relates the heart of God in the parable of the lost sheep. The shepherd leaves the ninety-nine and seeks the one who is lost. That is the heart of God. The resulting implication from this parable to church leadership is that when a sheep strays, they take priority over the ninety-nine who don't. It is also noteworthy that this passage on discipline is followed by Jesus' treatise on forgiveness (Matthew 18:21-35). This attitude must pervade the whole process.

We must logically conclude that following God's design is the best hope we have of drawing back a sinning member and also the means to protect the entire body from the stain of their sin. If we do not operate Biblically in this crucial area, we are acting as hirelings who tend the sheep when it is easy work, but run when the wolf comes to steal, kill, and destroy. If Satan, as a wolf, steals one of our sheep we must not stand idly by and say, "Oh well, there goes another one." It is a somber awareness when one admits, "But for the grace of God, that could be me." If I fell into sin, into some trap of the enemy, I would be grateful for spiritual leaders who would pursue me, who would leave the ninety-nine to seek me out.

    📖   Read James 5:14-15. How does God sometimes deal with hidden sin?

The Results Of How We Deal With Sin

When a church chooses to deal with sin in a Biblical manner two things result. First, the member is called into account for their sin. We are the body of Christ, the embrace of Christ, the servanthood of Christ. We also put flesh and blood on His discipline. When we call a sinning member to account, they see tangibly

PHILOSOPHY OF RESTORATION (CONTINUED)

the attitude of God toward their sin. This is a great responsibility, for we must show His justice and holiness, tempered with His mercy and compassion. How do we do that? By never moving beyond their sin until they recognize it and repent of it, while being quick to forgive when they do. The Spirit of God within us doesn't bless us in one area of our lives while we cling to sin in another. He continually draws our attention back to our sin until it is dealt with, and our walk goes no further until we do. In the case of the unrepentant, who it would appear have seared their conscience enough to be content not to respond to the conviction of the Spirit, the church becomes a second line of defense. We express visibly and physically what God is already saying. This continual reminder, this lasting call to repentance, is the best hope we have for restoring a sinning member.

Another resulting benefit of rightly exercising the discipline and restoration process is the purification of the church. *"A little leaven leavens the whole lump of dough."* By removing the leaven of a sinning, unrepentant member we purify the whole body. Certainly, we do not remove all sin from the body since *"we all stumble in many ways"* (James 3:2), but we make it clear to all that refusing to repent of sin is an unwelcome attitude. We make the body an uncomfortable place for the unrepentant. When I see someone else's sin dealt with in a serious manner, I take my own sin more seriously. When the body is free from rebellious believers, they stand out more clearly when they appear. If there is sin in the camp, all suffer the consequences. We see no example in Scripture of God overlooking the unrepentant and allowing them to continue in that state. We are called to the same commitment.

Conversely, if we do not deal fully and biblically with sin in our body, it becomes comfortable and acceptable to remain in an unrepentant state. All are encouraged to take their own sin less seriously and the whole body becomes less holy, less like Christ. Our testimony is compromised, and the name of Christ is defamed by our lack of respect for the holiness of God. As Paul quoted in Romans 2:24, *"The name of God is blasphemed among the Gentiles* [unbelievers] *because of you."* We cannot afford not to deal seriously with sin in the body for which we bear responsibility.

When Do the Elders Get Involved?

To summarize, not all discipline situations require the involvement of the elders of the church. Practically speaking, they should only be involved in two types of situations:

1. It is appropriate to involve the elders in a discipline situation when a properly confronted member of the body (as defined in Steps 1 through 4 of "the process of discipline") is unrepentant about a Biblically defined sin they are guilty of, or…

2. When a member of the body involved in a conflict with another person seeks Biblical/doctrinal advice.

In the case of an unrepentant member who has been properly confronted, although in some cases it may be appropriate to involve individual elders in Step 2, the elders as a whole do not get involved until Step 3, and then their involvement is in the form of binding discipline. In the case of members seeking Biblical/doctrinal advice, this may involve the elders as a whole or individual elders, and their involvement is in the form of non-binding counsel. To keep this system structurally practical and to keep it from absorbing the elders' attention and usurping their ministry function, the elder board should in each instance appoint/designate an elder/staff to be the key player to track with the situation as their representative, operating in their authority and reporting back to them. Usually, this person will already be identified by the situation, but when they are not, the elders should make such an appointment.

Philosophy of Restoration (Continued)

Notes:

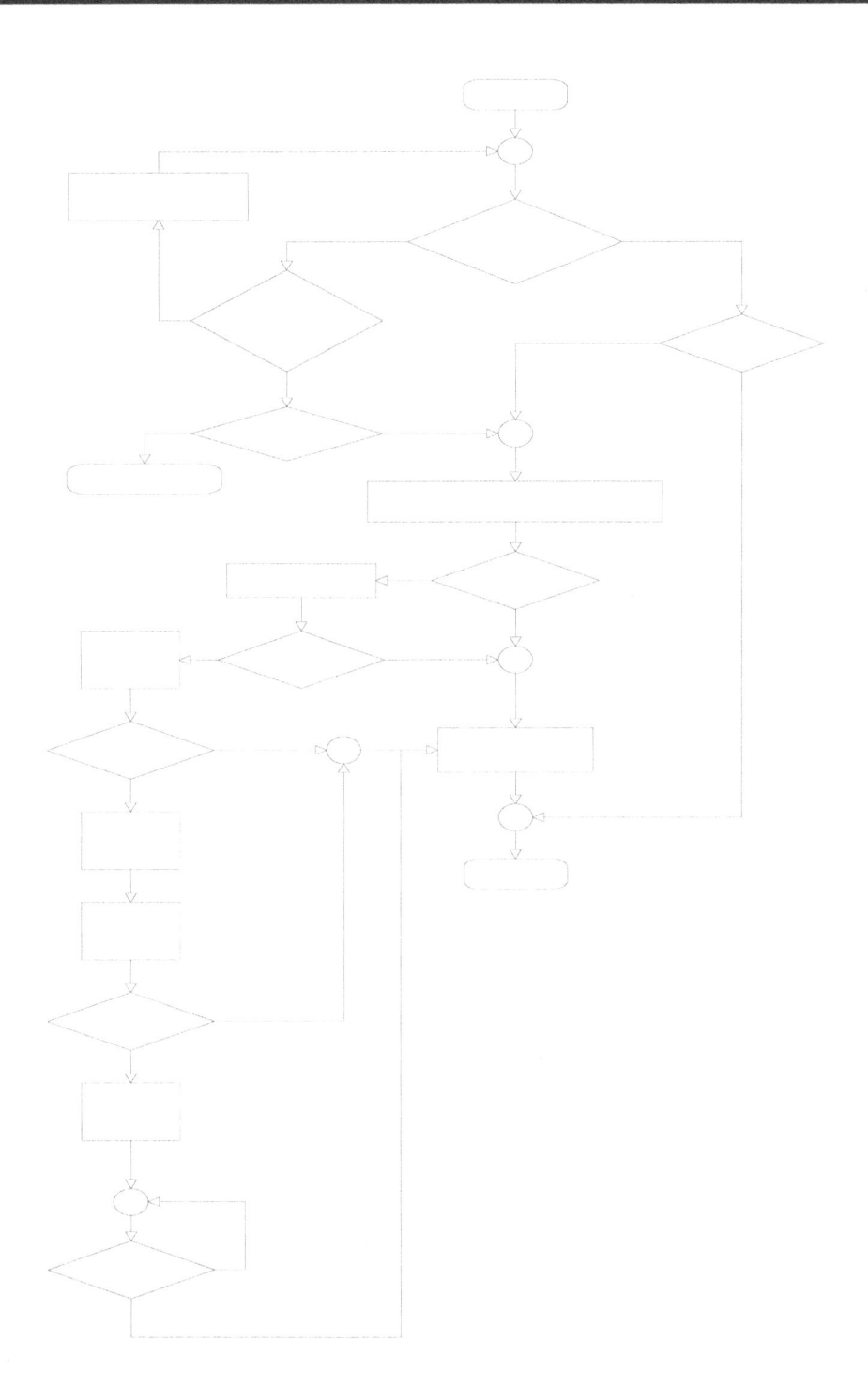

Philosophy of Restoration (Continued)

PHILOSOPHY OF RESTORATION – SAMPLE LETTERS

SAMPLES, JENNINGS & RAY, P.L.L.C.   *A PROFESSIONAL LIMITED LIABILITY COMPANY*
Attorneys and Counselors at Law
SHALLOWFORD LAW CENTER
130 JORDAN DRIVE
CHATTANOOGA, TENNESSEE 37421
423/892-2006 (telephone)
423/892-1919 (facsimile)

Hoyt O. Samples * (hsamples@sampleslaw.com)
Michael S. Jennings * (mjennings@sampleslaw.com)
Thomas E. Ray + (ray@raylegal.com)
Mitzi P. Samples (msamples@sampleslaw.com)
*licensed in Tennessee and Georgia
+Certified as a Business Bankruptcy and Consumer
Bankruptcy Specialist by the Tennessee Commission on
Continuing Legal Education and Specialization

April 26, 2004

Chattanooga, Tennessee

VIA CERTIFIED MAIL
RETURN RECEIPT REQUESTED
PERSONAL AND CONFIDENTIAL

Dear:

I have a heavy heart as I write this letter, but I have hope because of my faith in a sovereign Lord.

The General Council of Elders have followed with concern what has happened in your personal life as a result of your alcohol addiction.

As you know, Steve McCary, Steve Corley, myself and others have confronted you multiple occasions about this matter. Our last meeting as a group was in Steve McCary's office on March 17, 2004. In all of our meetings, you have been asked to demonstrate a heart that is truly repentant of your sinful conduct, together with conduct demonstrative of that repentance. Your conduct has consistently failed to match your words.

Attached is a position paper from Woodland Park Baptist Church on the Ministry of Restoration as followed in our church. Your initial contact with Steve Corley constituted Step One in the Restoration Process, and your subsequent meetings with myself, Steve McCary, and Steve Corley were all a part of Step Two of the Restoration Process. We are now at Step Three in this process.

The next Lord's Supper service is currently scheduled for May 23, 2004. At that time, we will, with much sorrow, bring your name before the church to enlist the prayers of the Body--as well as their involvement as the Lord leads--in calling you to repentance and restoration.

This course of action will not be taken, however, if you are willing to truly repent and turn from your sin pattern and seek genuine reconciliation with the Lord, as well as with your family. We know that reconciliation will require participation by and your children, and they may not be willing to immediately participate in that process. The loss of your family could well be a consequence of the path you have chosen. However, we are calling you as brothers in Christ to repentance and a right

Philosophy of Restoration – Sample Letters (Continued)

April 26, 2004
Page 2

relationship with Jesus Christ. We beg you to frankly consider the course you are now taking --either by action or non-action-- and turn from that path. We are duty bound, however, to follow the requirements of Matthew 18 if your heart remains hardened to your sin. At this time, we are asking you to (1) turn from your reliance on alcohol; (2) confess your sin, seeking restoration of your relationship with the Lord (I John 1:9); (3) accept a Biblical accountability process to demonstrate the genuineness of your repentance and to buttress your resolve; and (4) demonstrate your willingness to seek restoration of your relationship with your family. It is imperative that you take advantage of counseling that is available to you to evidence the seriousness of any stated desire for repentance and restoration.

We stand ready to help you. Please understand that our hearts' desire is for a restoration of your relationship with the Lord and--if the Lord permits--restoration of your marriage. This letter is not motivated by malice or spite. Instead, we desire to come alongside of you to help in this time of great difficulty for you and your family.

Please contact Steve McCary, Steve Corley, myself, or any other Elder or staff member to discuss this further. We anxiously await to hear from you. Nothing would personally please me more than to postpone any action on May 23 because you contact us after receiving this letter and commit to cooperate in this process.

Faithfully yours,

Michael S. Jennings
For the General Council of Elders

MSJ:rsd

bcc: General Council of Elders
Mr. Steve McCary
Mr. Steve Corley

bbcc: File of WPBC

PHILOSOPHY OF RESTORATION – SAMPLE LETTERS (CONTINUED)

████████ —STEP 3

CORRECTIVE DISCIPLINE (Matthew 18:15–17)
LORD'S SUPPER, May 23, 2004

Since its adoption on May 11, 1988, the Woodland Park Baptist Church <u>Constitution and Bylaws</u> has called for the use of corrective discipline where necessary to bring a member in sin to the point of spiritual restoration. In an effort to fully implement this process here at Woodland Park, a formal membership meeting was called on October 31, 1993. At that time, our <u>Constitution and Bylaws</u> was amended to clarify the Church's position on the ministry of restoration, as outlined in the eighteenth chapter of the Gospel of Matthew.

Since that time, our church leadership has been involved in several situations where the process of corrective discipline has been instituted in an effort to restore a sinning member of this body to a right spiritual relationship.

The first two steps of this process of restoration are of necessity a private process. We, therefore, are not at liberty to share with you how members' lives can and have been changed by being called to account for sin in their lives. However, we now have a situation that has developed to the point where Matthew 18:17a requires us to "*...tell it to the church: ...*"

[READ MATTHEW 18:15–17]

Matt 18:15 (NASB) *"And if your brother sins, go and reprove him in private; if he listens to you, you have won your brother.*
16 *"But if he does not listen [to you,] take one or two more with you, so that by the mouth of two or three witnesses every fact may be confirmed.*
17 *"And if he refuses to listen to them, tell it to the church; and if he refuses to listen even to the church, let him be to you as a Gentile and a tax-gatherer.*

████████ joined Woodland Park Baptist Church in February, 1988. ████ has been involved in an unbiblical activity and lifestyle over a period of time involving habitual use of alcohol. ████ has been confronted with his personal Biblical responsibility to the Lord, and has rejected repeated overtures from members of this body as well as from the staff and elders. ████ has chosen not to repent of his conduct and seek restoration of relationship with the Lord, but rather to continue in this unbiblical activity.

Because ████ has refused to submit to the authority of the Scriptures—by refusing to respond to oral and written requests to meet the church leadership and either provide biblical justification for his actions or repent of his unbiblical conduct—the elders of the church have chosen, in obedience to the Word of God, to bring this issue to the congregation.

Min. of Restoration, step 3, form B -- p. 1

SERVANT APPROACH LEADERSHIP TRAINING: Building Biblical Philosophy

PHILOSOPHY OF RESTORATION – SAMPLE LETTERS (CONTINUED)

SAMPLES, JENNINGS, RAY & CLEM, P.L.L.C.   A PROFESSIONAL LIMITED LIABILITY COMPANY
Attorneys and Counselors at Law
SHALLOWFORD LAW CENTER
130 JORDAN DRIVE
CHATTANOOGA, TENNESSEE 37421
423/892-2006 (telephone)
423/892-1919 (facsimile)

Hoyt O. Samples * (hsamples@sampleslaw.com)
Michael S. Jennings * (mjennings@sampleslaw.com)
Thomas E. Ray + (ray@raylegal.com)
J. Christopher Clem * (cclem@sampleslaw.com)
Mitzi P. Samples (msamples@sampleslaw.com)
*licensed in Tennessee and Georgia
+Certified as a Business Bankruptcy and Consumer
Bankruptcy Specialist by the Tennessee Commission on
Continuing Legal Education and Specialization

September 15, 2004

Chattanooga, Tennessee

VIA HAND DELIVERY
PERSONAL AND CONFIDENTIAL

Dear

With this letter I am delivering to you a copy of the statement read to our church membership at the conclusion of our Lord's Supper Service on May 23, 2004.

Our sole purpose in sharing this information with the congregation has been to obey Matthew 18 and to enlist the prayer of the Body on your behalf.

We genuinely desire to come alongside you to provide accountability and counseling as may be necessary to restore a healthy relationship with the Lord. Please call myself, Steve McCary, Steve Corley, or anyone here in leadership at WPBC, to discuss these issues further.

Our next Lord's Supper is scheduled for October 3, 2004. If this issue remains unresolved at that time, we will have no alternative but to follow the Scriptural mandate (Matthew 18) to treat you "as a Gentile and a tax gatherer." The intent here is not to ridicule or embarrass you, but Scripture will require that we actually break fellowship with you. The same concept is reiterated by Paul in II Thessalonians 3:6, 14-15.

You are my friend. Please reconsider the road you are traveling.

Faithfully yours,

Michael S. Jennings
For the Firm

MSJ:rsd

bcc: Elders
        Steve McCary
        Steve Corley

bbcc: File of Church Discipline

Philosophy of Restoration – Sample Letters (Continued)

▇▇▇▇▇—STEP 4

CORRECTIVE DISCIPLINE (Matthew 18:15–17)
LORD'S SUPPER, October 3, 2004

Since its adoption on May 11, 1988, the Woodland Park Baptist Church <u>Constitution and Bylaws</u> has called for the use of corrective discipline where necessary to bring a member in sin to the point of spiritual restoration. In an effort to fully implement this process here at Woodland Park, a formal membership meeting was called on October 31, 1993. At that time, our <u>Constitution and Bylaws</u> was amended to clarify the Church's position on the ministry of restoration, as outlined in the eighteenth chapter of the Gospel of Matthew. Since that time, our church leadership has been involved in many situations where the process of corrective discipline has been instituted in an effort to restore a sinning member to the body.

This process of restoration begins, by necessity, as a private process. Matthew 18:15 states: *"And if your brother sins, go and reprove him in private; ..."* The text literally says, *"...between you and him alone."* This is the first step of corrective discipline, and Matthew tells us, *"...if he listens to you, you have won your brother."* The second step is related in verse 16: *"But if he does not listen to you, take one or two more with you, so that by the mouth of two or three witnesses every fact may be confirmed."* Gratefully, most of the situations where corrective discipline has been instituted by our church have been resolved in these first two steps.

However, on May 23, 2004, at the Lord's Supper, we informed you of a situation that had developed beyond those first two steps. Matthew 18:17 defines the third step in corrective discipline like this: *"And if he refuses to listen to them* (the two or more witnesses), *tell it to the church; ..."* In order to fulfill our Biblical responsibility, we informed you at that time that ▇▇▇ ▇▇▇, a member since February, 1988, had engaged in an unbiblical activity and lifestyle over a period of time involving habitual use of alcohol. Despite repeated overtures from members of this church, including staff and elders, ▇▇▇ had not repented of his actions, nor did he seek restoration of his relationship with the Lord, but chose rather to continue in this unbiblical activity.

Because of ▇▇▇'s refusal to submit to the authority of the Scriptures—by refusing to meet the church leadership and either provide Biblical justification for his actions or to repent of his unbiblical conduct—on May 23, 2004 the elders of the church brought this issue to the congregation for the purpose of enlisting the prayer and involvement of the body. It is with great sadness and regret that we now inform you that even this third step has failed to produce restoration.

Because of ▇▇▇'s continued refusal to respond to oral and written requests, we now must move to the fourth step in this process. Matthew 18:17 directs us: *"...and if he refuses to listen even to the church, let him be to you as a Gentile and a tax-gatherer."* Essentially, Jesus says to treat him as an unbeliever, as one outside the body of Christ. This command of the Lord requires us to formally break fellowship with ▇▇▇▇▇ and to rescind his membership in this congregation. In 2 Thessalonians 3:6, Paul instructs us: *"Now we command you, brethren, in the name of our*

Min. of Restoration, step 4 -- p. 1

PHILOSOPHY OF RESTORATION – SAMPLE LETTERS (CONTINUED)

Lord Jesus Christ, that you keep aloof from every brother who leads an unruly life and not according to the tradition which you received from us." Verses 14 and 15 clarify further: *"And if anyone does not obey our instruction in this letter* (Scripture), *take special note of that man and do not associate with him, so that he may be put to shame. And yet do not regard him as an enemy, but admonish him as a brother."* It is still our hope that at some point in the future, ▓▓ will repent so that he might be restored to the fellowship of the body, and we admonish you to pray for that to occur. In the meantime, you should avoid any contact with ▓▓, except for those contacts designed to minister to him and to draw him into fellowship with God.

_____   _____
(Rev. John Meador)   (W. Roger Fitch)

_____   _____
(Dr. Spiros Zodhiates)   (Michael S. Jennings)

_____   _____
(Dr. Robert Westcott)   (Charles T. Weaver)

_____   _____
(Rev. Haywood Cosby)   (John Rankin)

Min. of Restoration, step 4 -- p. 2

Philosophy of Restoration – Sample Letters (Continued)

The purpose of sharing this information with the congregation is to enlist the prayer of the body, as well as your involvement as the Lord leads, in calling ▓▓▓▓ to repentance. Our purpose is certainly not to shame, ridicule, or humiliate ▓▓▓. We are mindful that we all have "feet of clay," and "there but for the grace of God" we might each find ourselves with an unsubmissive or rebellious spirit. It is therefore in a spirit of soberness and with an attitude of self-examination that we request that each member of this congregation not engage in private discussions about ▓▓, but instead pray earnestly for the restoration of our brother in Christ.

_____
(Rev. John Meador)

_____
(W. Roger Fitch)

_____
(Dr. Spiros Zodhiates)

_____
(Michael S. Jennings)

_____
(Dr. Robert Westcott)

_____
(Charles T. Weaver)

Min. of Restoration, step 3, form B -- p. 2

SERVANT APPROACH LEADERSHIP TRAINING: Building Biblical Philosophy   (revised 2/20/223)

SESSION 6: HOMEWORK SUMMARY

Due Date: _____

Review of homework assignments:

Philosophy of Women in Leadership

© Copyright 2002 Eddie Rasnake
You may reproduce this chapter at no charge as long as proper credit is given and no changes are made to the document.

Women are important to the plan of God. This may seem like an unnecessary statement of the obvious, yet often this important message gets clouded by our culture. There are even those in the body of Christ that so promote an imbalanced view of submission, that they leave little room for women to do anything in the service of God except take care of the nursery. Yet God makes it clear that women are important to Him.

In Genesis 1:26-28, when the Trinity initiated the creation of mankind, we read, *"Then God said, 'Let Us make man in Our image, according to Our likeness; and let <u>THEM</u> rule over the fish of the sea and over the birds of the sky and over the cattle and over all the earth, and over every creeping thing that creeps on the earth.' God created man in His own image, in the image of God He created him; male and female He created <u>THEM</u>. God blessed them; and God said to <u>THEM</u>, 'Be fruitful and multiply, and fill the earth, and subdue it; and rule over the fish of the sea and over the birds of the sky and over every living thing that moves on the earth.'"* (emphasis mine). In the plan of God, it takes both male and female to reflect His image and rule His creation.

During the dismal period of the Judges, it was Deborah who God used in a mighty way to deliver His people (Judges 4 & 5) and who was called a prophetess (Judges 4:4). Huldah spoke, *"Thus says the Lord,"* just as the male prophets did (2 Kings 22:14; 2 Chron. 34:22). It was Miriam, the sister of Moses, who ministered alongside him and was also called a prophetess (Ex. 15:20-21) as was the wife of the prophet Isaiah (Is. 8:3). Anna in the New Testament was called a prophetess (Luke 2:36). God used the woman Rahab to save the lives of the two spies Joshua sent into Canaan (Joshua 2). Young Esther was God's chosen agent to save all the Jews from extermination (Esther 4:13-17). It was a woman who rescued the infant Joash from wicked queen Athaliah's evil attempt to destroy all the descendants of David, the line from which the Messiah would come (2 Chron. 22:10-12). In fact, as we read the genealogy of Jesus, we find five women mentioned there, contrary to the normal culture of mentioning only the male descendants (Mt. 1:2-16). God values and uses women, plain and simple.

When God became flesh and dwelt among us, He stepped forward as the great liberator of women. Jesus affirmed women in His public ministry. He reached out to the Samaritan woman at the well (John 4), and then used her to take the gospel to a whole village. He rescued the woman caught in adultery from unjust justice (John 8). He gave women a prominence in His life and ministry that the culture did not.

In the ministry of the apostle Paul, we see example after example of women stepping forward and being used by God. It was Eunice and Lois, probably converts of Paul's at Lystra, who laid the spiritual foundation of one of his key disciples, Timothy (1 Tim. 1:5). It was Pricilla who along with her husband Aquilla labored alongside Paul in Corinth (Acts 18). This same couple (with the wife mentioned first suggesting a prominence to her labor) came alongside Apollos and corrected some doctrinal mistakes (Acts 18:26).

What is the message from all of this? Women are important to God. If they weren't He wouldn't have made so many. In fact, often women are far more spiritually sensitive and responsive than men. It is time for the church to affirm their contributions to the cause of Christ. Whatever we conclude about the role of women in the church, we must affirm the Biblical message that they are of equal worth to God. Galatians 3:26-27 makes it clear that slaves and free persons may hold different positions in society, but they are of equal value in God's sight. Likewise, male and female are *"one in Christ Jesus."*

SERVANT APPROACH LEADERSHIP TRAINING: Building Biblical Philosophy

PHILOSOPHY OF WOMEN IN LEADERSHIP (CONTINUED)

What is the place of Women in Leadership?

Whenever the subject is mentioned of the proper place of women in leadership and church life, invariably Paul's words to Timothy come up. It is important before you look at exactly what Paul said that we recognize the context of those words. Paul's first letter to Timothy was written to help his disciple bring order to a church in disarray. In 1 Timothy 3:15 we read, *"…I write so that you will know how one ought to conduct himself in the household of God."* In this context of dialog about public worship, Paul addresses women teaching and learning in the church.

  As you look at 1 Timothy 3:11, do you think Paul is speaking to Timothy regarding women as leaders or regarding wives of leaders?

Why do you think that?

There are many reasons why each person believes what they believe. Look at the list below and place in order from 1-4 (1 being most significant) these different reasons for what you believe about women in leadership.

___ I think women are not given enough prominence in the church.
___ What I believe is based on the traditions of our church.
___ What I believe is based on what I have been taught by others.
___ What I believe is based on having thoroughly studied the relevant passages.

When one looks closely at 1 Timothy 3:11 in its context, it is most likely referring to the wives of the deacons, not a separate office of deaconess since the qualifications for a deacon continue in verse 12 and include *"husbands of only one wife"*. If Paul saw deacons as being either men or women, he would probably have said something like "married to only one person." One would expect that if Paul were referring to a different office (deaconess), he would have finished the one before beginning the other as he did with elders. This does not necessarily close the door on women as deacons, but it doesn't fully open it either. Let's look at some other passages.

  Look at Romans 16:1. Do you think Phoebe is a deaconess based on this?

Can a woman be a deacon? While some see in these brief passages room for allowing it, the issue is far from being clearly affirmed Scripturally. Equally important, even if you believe these Scriptures allow the practice, you must recognize that there are a great many who do not. It would present an extra challenge for a woman to be an effective leader while also being a stumbling block to some in the body she would serve. Jesus was a great liberator of women. He afforded them a prominence and value the culture did not. But he did not place any women among His disciples – His leaders in training (see Mt. 10:1-4; Mk. 3:13-19; Lk. 6:12-16). He ministered to and was ministered to by women (see Mt. 27:55) – in fact, a group of women were His primary financial supporters (Lk. 8:1-3) – but He did not make them leaders over men.

Philosophy of Women in Leadership (Continued)

Can a Woman Teach in the church?

When the apostle Paul wrote Timothy about conduct in *"the household of God"* (1 Timothy 3:15) he didn't leave out the topic of women teaching. It is separate from the question of whether or not a woman can be an elder or a deacon, but it is related to it. If a woman cannot teach in church, she cannot be an elder. What is God's view of this issue?

Culturally, our day is awash in messages that blur the God-given distinctions between men and women. Though the physical differences are obvious, many try to argue that those are the only differences. It is important that we interpret our experiences and our culture in the light of Scripture, instead of the other way around. Some today are trying to remove the concept of the Fatherhood of God, not because it isn't clearly taught in the Bible, but because it disagrees with their cultural bias. The Bible must be our authority.

📖 Read through 1 Timothy 2:9-15.

What does Paul say a woman should do in church?

What does he say she should not do?

Why?

Paul instructs that in church (that is the preceding context of the chapter) a woman should be modestly and discreetly dressed (see also 1 Pet. 3:1-4). She should make her reputation by good works, not good looks. She is to receive instruction with a submissive attitude. She is not allowed to *"teach or exercise authority"* over a man. This does not say she cannot teach. The Greek word *didasko* (translated "teach") here is in the present tense, meaning teaching in an ongoing basis. The text does not say a woman can never teach, but rather, should not teach men on a regular basis. Paul gives several reasons for this limitation. First, he affirms that God in His sovereignty chose to create man first. This does not mean greater value, but unique purpose. Woman was created to be a helper to man – not the other way around. Second, Paul argues that it was Eve who first disobeyed God, not Adam. Moreover, her disobedience was because of deception. It is difficult to define all that is meant by this, but the main point is clear. Eve was susceptible to deception leading to sin, while Adam sinned willfully.

While traditionally the church has emphasized the restrictions of this passage, to treat it fairly we must acknowledge that the main point is one of liberation, not restriction. Paul's words do not appear in a vacuum. They exist in a cultural context far different than ours today. Typically, in the culture of the day, women were not taught or allowed to learn. Some Jewish rabbis would not teach women at all, and some called it "throwing pearls to pigs." The woman's place in the Gentile world was not much better. Yet the

PHILOSOPHY OF WOMEN IN LEADERSHIP (CONTINUED)

central imperative of this passage is not the restriction on teaching. The lone imperative (command) is to *"receive instruction"* or as the KJV translates it, *"Let the woman learn…"* In the context of that culture Paul's words are a positive, not a negative thing. The admonition against taking an ongoing position of teacher was juxtaposed against this positive invitation for women to be included in the times of instruction as equal learners. It is not an imperative (command) but rather, an indicative (statement of fact). Paul says, *"But I do not allow a woman to teach or exercise authority over a man, but to remain quiet."* Paul is contrasting what he does allow (women to learn) with what he does not allow (women to teach or exercise authority over men).

Finally, Paul makes the statement that women are *"preserved through the bearing of children."* Now, what does that mean? The Greek word translated *"preserved"* can refer to salvation, though it doesn't always carry an eternal connotation. There have been several different interpretations put forward over the years. One view is that Paul is not speaking of women in general but specifically has Mary in view – in other words, he is contrasting sin entering the world through Eve with salvation entering the world through Mary. It is an interesting idea, but if that were the point one would expect it to be made more clearly. Another view is that eternal salvation is what is meant. In this view women are not *"saved by means of childbearing"*, but "saved in the midst of childbearing" or "in spite of" childbearing (whose additional pain stands as being their unique consequence from the fall). The third view is that salvation is only in a temporal sense. In context, women are seen as being saved from all limitations on teaching through being given the primary role of teaching in the home with her children. This idea would make more sense contextually.

 📖 What does Titus 2:3-5 indicate about women teaching?

Paul makes clear in Titus 2 that women can and should teach. Therefore, the restriction in 1 Timothy cannot be taken to limit all teaching. Trying to take authority over men seems to be the main point there. Older women are to teach younger women how to be good wives, mothers, and Christians.

The church needs women. Their service is greatly needed. Their voice should be heard and valued. But they are subject to limitations as are all in the body of Christ. Submission is not always by an inferior to a superior (as in children to parents) but sometimes is used of one of equal value placing themselves under the authority of another. Most of the men in a congregation are not elders. They too must submit to leaders. All of us must be submissive to the head of the church, Christ.

* For additional thoughts on the role of women in teaching read the Doctrinal Commentary by eminent Greek Scholar, Dr. Spiros Zodhiates in his comments on 1 Timothy 2:9-15 *The Complete Word Study New Testament*, (Chattanooga, TN: AMG Publishers).

PHILOSOPHY OF WOMEN IN LEADERSHIP (CONTINUED)

Notes:

Philosophy of Retreats and Conferences

© Copyright 1998, 2005 Eddie Rasnake

You may reproduce this chapter at no charge as long as proper credit is given and no changes are made to the document.

The Biblical Basis for Retreats and Conferences

Retreats and conferences are not a unique invention of our era, and they aren't something humans created. Retreats and conferences have been a part of spiritual life since before the time of Christ. At least four times a year, devout Jews would pack up and go to Jerusalem for a spiritual retreat or conference. Now, they didn't call them retreats, but in function they operated much the same way as our modern retreats or conferences. These gatherings, usually either a feast or a festival, were essential to Jewish spirituality and became significant milestones in their relationship with God. The major feasts and festivals commemorated significant events in Israel's history and lasted anywhere from several days to a week or more. For example, the celebration of the Passover was a lengthy observance. Other holy gatherings included the "Feast of Booths," "Yom Kippur" (the day of atonement), "Pentecost," etc. Each of these spiritual events, which were scattered throughout the calendar year, roughly parallel the function of our modern-day spiritual retreats and conferences.

Distinctives of a Good Retreat

What distinguishes a retreat from a conference? Practically speaking, the main difference between a retreat and a conference is not length of time, but focus. A retreat is focused primarily on refreshment and renewal in our personal relationship with God. A conference on the other hand, is much more prescriptive and focuses on a specific area or areas of our walk and ministry.

- Read Mark 1:32-39 and answer the following questions:

    ♦ What time was it that Jesus began healing the people?

    ♦ How many people wanted to see Jesus?

    ♦ How many people did Jesus *actually* deal with?

    ♦ What was Jesus' top priority the next day?

    ♦ What environment were they in at the moment?

    ♦ What environment did they need?

    ♦ What was the purpose of their retreat?

PHILOSOPHY OF RETREATS AND CONFERENCES (CONTINUED)

- ♦ How long did their retreat last?

- ♦ Read Mark 3:7-10 and identify the similarities with the above passage.

The Role of the Small Group

Often one of the components of a retreat or conference is the use of the small group. Sometimes it is employed for training purposes. Breaking the larger group into smaller ones enables equipping to target several different levels of maturity and need. It can be applied more directly to exactly where a person is. Another use of small groups in such settings is for the purpose of relationship and interaction. Whatever the structure, these smaller groups give greater opportunity for ministry.

As we look at the ministry model of Jesus, it is obvious He didn't limit Himself to a single communication vehicle. His repertoire ranged in degrees from preaching to the multitudes all the way down to working with people one-on-one. He spent a considerable amount of time in this range with His small group that we refer to as "The Twelve." Although they are often a part of retreats and conferences, small groups are not limited to that venue. Whether pulling aside for a special event, or gathering regularly, we see in small groups the same theme played out: separation and focus.

Although it is possible to make mistakes by scheduling the retreat or conference at the wrong time, the biggest mistake you can make is not planning them at all. They are a very strategic tool in ministry.

Read Mark 6:7-13;30-32 and answer the following questions:

- ♦ What had the disciples just been doing when we get to verse 30?

- ♦ What environment were they in at the moment?

- ♦ What environment did they need?

- ♦ What was the purpose of their retreat?

- ♦ How long did their retreat last?

- ♦ Read Mark 3:7-10 and identify the similarities with the above passage.

THE PRINCIPLE OF SEPARATION

Dr. Robert E. Coleman makes the following observations on how small groups and retreats go hand-in-hand in his *The Master Plan of Evangelism*:

SERVANT APPROACH LEADERSHIP TRAINING: Building Biblical Philosophy

PHILOSOPHY OF RETREATS AND CONFERENCES (CONTINUED)

> Frequently [Jesus] would take them with him on a retreat to some mountainous area of the country where he was relatively unknown, seeking to avoid publicity as far as possible. They took trips together to Tyre and Sidon to the northwest (Mark 7:24; Matt. 15:21; to the "borders of Decapolis" (Mark 7:31, cf., Matt. 15:29) and "the parts of Dalmanutha" to the southeast of Galilee (Mark 8:10; cf., Matt. 15:39); and to the "villages of Caesarea Philippi" to the northeast (Mark 8:27; cf., Matt. 16:13). These journeys were made partly because of the opposition of the Pharisees and the hostility of Herod, but primarily because Jesus felt the need to get alone with his disciples. Later he spent several months with his disciples in Perea, east of the Jordan (Luke 13:22-19:28; John 10:40-11:54; Matt. 19:1-20:34; Mark 10:1-52). As opposition mounted there, Jesus "walked no more openly among the Jews, but departed thence into the country near to the wilderness, into a city called Ephraim; and there he tarried with his disciples" (John 11:54). When at the last the time came for him to go to Jerusalem, he significantly "took the twelve disciples apart" from the rest as he made his way slowly to the city (Matt 20:17; cf., Mark 10:32).

The principle of separation isn't limited to geography. The distinction of the small group is that they separate themselves from the main throng for a focused time together. When we see this modeled by Christ, it was for the purpose of *training*. This is in contrast to His approach with the multitudes, where His purpose was informing. This principle was so ingrained into His disciples that we see it still practiced many years later (e.g., Paul's entourage of "companions" [Acts 13:13] such as Timothy, Silas, Luke, John Mark, Erastus, Sopater, Aristarchus, Secundus, Gaius, Tychicus, Trophimus). You can see the principle passed on in 2 Timothy 2:2 when Paul refers to the faithful men.

THE PRINCIPLE OF FOCUS

As mentioned above, the small group approach is based on focus rather than size. The smaller environment allows you to focus on training and allows a controlled environment. A small group should meet often enough to build "community." Accountability becomes a natural extension as peer relationships are built. As members open up and share, they also promote openness to both rebuke and encouragement. Training is reinforced since they learn from both their leader and their peers.

While size isn't the critical factor of the small group, it does play a role. If the group is too large, you'll end up with spectators instead of participants. If the group is too small, you might not have the diversity and the balance of spiritual gifts to meet the needs of the group. A smaller size also allows a leader to create a controlled environment—an environment for success. As the group begins to apply their training, a manageable membership lets you both assist and evaluate their progress.

Evaluation is a vital part of the small group. In a small group a leader can identify leadership candidates. As a discipler, you want to be on the lookout for spiritual giftedness, skill levels, and commitment. Evaluation takes time, so a small group needs to meet often enough and long enough to build community and to allow each member's true character to surface.

THE PRINCIPLE OF SELECTIVITY

Since a leader pours significant time and energy into a small group, you don't want that effort wasted. A leader must be selective in both material and membership. There are two main types of small groups—the open group and the closed group. The open group is available to "whosoever will." It requires no special invitation and offers flexibility to come and go as one desires. The membership of such groups is constantly changing. This type of group provides an important dynamic, especially in the early stages of growth. The closed group requires a more defined commitment. It both asks more of its members and

PHILOSOPHY OF RETREATS AND CONFERENCES (CONTINUED)

offers more to them. A closed group requires an invitation and necessitates a defined commitment. Jesus and the twelve is a good Biblical example of a closed group. Jesus "appointed" them and formalized the relationship. They could not simply decide to sleep in one morning and not participate. Jesus was committing Himself to them, and he required commitment from them in like measure.

As a group evolves from open to closed, the principle of selectivity becomes more relevant. It takes time for each member's true commitment and character to surface. If a member is lacking in commitment or character, they won't benefit from the small group environment. In addition, they will have a detrimental effect on the rest of the members if they remain in the group. You'll need to minister to unqualified believers via a different vehicle. At a glance, the idea of a closed group seems to lack grace and to play favorites. I was once accused of cult-like behavior by someone who was offended by our offering of closed groups. They thought anyone should be allowed to participate in the group if they so desired. Clearly that was not the way the twelve disciples functioned.

 Read Mark 3:14,15 and Luke 6:12-13. How did Christ demonstrate the principles of separation, focus, and selectivity in these passages?

- Separation:

- Focus:

- Selectivity:

What fruit came of His closed group?

Jesus always operated from a plan. Everything He did was intentional. He appointed the twelve to be with Him, but He expected them to become ready to be sent out. To some it may seem uncompassionate to exclude the spiritually unhealthy and those not ready for strong commitment from the inner group. In the long run, however, this is the most compassionate thing we can do. The best hope we have of meeting the needs of the spiritual novices and all the spiritually sick is to multiply ourselves into the spiritually healthy and make them into ministers as well. Not doing so, guarantees that the number of weak and immature we minister to will never grow beyond what it is now. On the other hand, by closing off part of our ministry time, we can build leaders so that each year more can be ministered to. One of the greatest benefits of retreats and conferences is that at least for the weekend you have a closed group of people who are there because they want to be. This is the greatest place to focus your attention.

Philosophy of Retreats and Conferences (Continued)

Notes:

Philosophy of Beginning a New Ministry

© Copyright 1992, 2005 Eddie Rasnake
You may reproduce this chapter at no charge as long as proper credit is given and no changes are made to the document.

Because the church is an organism rather than an organization, it is constantly recreating itself. Your church may have met at the same location for a hundred years, but it is not the same church it was a hundred years ago. In fact, it is not the same church it was two or three years ago. Try leaving your church for two or three years and then come back. You will discover that contrary to your desire, while you were gone it didn't stay in a time warp. People have changed. Some have died, and some have been born. Some you knew have left, and new people have come in to take their place. Even those who stay are different. Some have seen significant growth. Others may have seen their zeal grow cold. A church is never static. Much like the human body, cells are constantly dying as well as being born. The body as a whole is still there, but it is in a constant state of change. If it has exercised and eaten well, it is healthier. If not, well, that is reflected too. The same principle of change is true of the community in which your church exists. What does this have to do with beginning new ministries? Everything. One of the signs of a healthy church is the regular birth of new ministries, as well as the regular death of ministries which have run their course and served their purpose. This is what enables the church to continue to be relevant in a rapidly changing culture. Change will happen. The lack of change in the programs and practices of the church, still results in change. When programs and approaches are set in the immovable concrete of "We always did it that way," what changes is the influence that church has on the world around it. An unchanging church becomes marginalized by the changes in the culture around it and is decreasingly effective at reaching its community and culture. A healthy church recognizes the inevitability of change and manages this process in an intentional way. It recognizes change as a friend, and not an enemy. A healthy church is regularly celebrating the birth of new ministries.

Though beginning new ministries is inevitable in a changing world, one major issue must be settled before a church tackles these new beginnings. What are its distinctives, its core values? I am amazed at the number of churches around us that have no clear focus for why they exist. These churches are very busy with activity, but there is no real productivity. They are "doing church" instead of being the body of Christ. Their primary goal is maintaining their activities and keeping the thing running, but there is no sense of where it is going. Without a clear sense of where you are going, of what God has uniquely called your church to do and be, you are at the mercy of the latest fad or hand-me-down strategy that draws a crowd. What I have witnessed over and over is that what worked at another church "over there" may not work at my church. Approaches that do work often need adapting to fit the unique personality of another church. Jerry Cook stated it well: *"One thing working all kinds of devastation in the life of the church is the failure of the leadership to have a solid philosophy — a well-defined concept of how a church ought to operate and why"* (Jerry Cook, *"Love, Acceptance, and Forgiveness: Equipping the Church to Be Truly Christian in a Non-Christian World,"* Ventura, CA, Regal Books, 1979, p.23). Without a clearly defined philosophy and the core values and distinctives that flow out of it, a church has no way of evaluating someone's idea for a new ministry and whether it fits who they are and where they are headed. Ministries born out of such ambiguity often do as much damage to the overall ministry of a church as they do good. It is for this reason that step one in beginning a new ministry is to make sure the core values, Biblical philosophy and local distinctives have been identified and considered. This is not only helpful in determining if a new ministry is needed or will fit, but also makes it easy to say "No" to programs or strategies that don't fit.

If God is initiating a new ministry in your church or in THE church, let me share some practical steps to take, in order to do all that you can to help this new venture succeed. In a sense, a new ministry is like a small business. Historically most of those fail. The reason isn't usually because the idea wasn't right, but

PHILOSOPHY OF BEGINNING A NEW MINISTRY (CONTINUED)

because the process wasn't managed properly. The same principle holds true with starting a new ministry. If you want to do all that you can to help this new work succeed, you will need to follow this process in this order.

Personal Preparation

♦ **Define your vision, values and objectives.** Before a vision can be cast, it must be created. Awareness of a need is not enough. Anyone can identify a problem, but it takes leadership to implement an effective solution. Make a continuing and regular commitment to seeking God for direction. Map your objectives out as specifically as possible. Part of this process is to remember that your vision is a "part" and not the whole. In the context of a local church, it is one ministry that must weave together with all the other ministries so that together they can accomplish more than would be possible separately. To succeed, you must define your vision, values and objectives in a manner compatible with those of your church—any new ministry must be consistent with the established vision, values and objectives. While you must allow yourself time for balancing the whole counsel of Scripture on the area the new ministry addresses, you must also allow the main leaders of the church that same time to do so. The more you can anticipate their questions and concerns and address those up front, the more you can streamline the process. It is essential that all of your leadership personnel are operating off of the same page, and that page must be in the Bible.

  Look at Matthew 12:25 and identify what it has to say about a common philosophy and common objective.

♦ **Defer to Spiritual Authority.** Involve those whose participation or support are required and make sure their opinions and priorities are included. This means working the idea through the chain of command. It is hard to succeed without the support of other believers. In a local church this would mean meeting with the pastors and church lay leaders to share the burden and plan. Any new ministry would find it hard to succeed without their support, but even if that were possible, it would not be healthy. It would likely conflict with, and even work against the other priorities of the organization. We see this principle modeled in the early church in the verses below.

  Read Acts 6:1-7 and answer the questions below about how this new ministry was begun.

  a. Where did the idea originate?

  b. Who gave shape to the vision?

  c. What were the criteria for leaders and who set those?

  d. Who had responsibility to implement the vision?

  e. What was the priority of leadership?

  f. What is the significance of verse 6?

  g. What was the result of the plan?

PHILOSOPHY OF BEGINNING A NEW MINISTRY (CONTINUED)

Understand that there should always be willingness and desire on the part of leadership to see new ministries initiated and birthed on a grass-roots level, but they can't do everything. God often speaks to us through our burdens and therefore, the best person to begin a ministry is not the professional with the most training, but the person with the burden. At our church, the general rule is "if it is your burden, don't pass the responsibility to someone else." That sense of burden from the Lord is His means of putting the baton in your hands.

♦ **Dream dependently.** Make sure the idea has an element of faith. Dream as big as what God can do rather than limiting your vision to what you can do. Depend on Him and don't be satisfied with merely what you can do for God. Trust Him for the things which only He can do. It is important though that you do not dream independently. Ideas that originate with us instead of God will not have His blessing. He only anoints what He initiates.

 Now take a look at Acts 13:1-3.

  a. Who called the men to the mission task?

  b. To whom did the Lord reveal this call?

  c. What was the leadership's role in the call to Barnabas and Saul?

♦ **Determine your Priorities** – what needs to happen first? If there is not a prescribed deadline, I have always found it helpful to start with the end product and work my way backward step-by-step, identifying what it will take to get there.

♦ **Develop your Strategies** for each objective. What resources will it take? How many laborers are needed? Who has to be sold on the need? How can the objective be broken down into manageable steps? Part of your strategy must be the initial and ongoing training needed for the ministry to succeed.

 Read Ephesians 4:11-12 and identify the responsibilities and roles both of church leaders and laity in the functioning of a ministry.

♦ **Deploy the Ministry.** Implement your vision…

Progressively (the way to eat an elephant is one bite at a time)

Strategically (make your shots count – you have limited time and ammo)

Evaluatively (Continue to evaluate and redefine your vision and objectives as you go. If something worked, make sure you know why. If something isn't working, make sure you know why. Even if something is working, keep looking for ways to make it better).

Philosophy of Beginning a New Ministry (Continued)

The first step in deploying a properly prepared new ministry is...

Public Invitation

1. Cast Vision – The congregation or community has to be convinced of...

♦ The reality of the need (You have seen it or you wouldn't be here. Many others have not seen it or a solution would have already been proposed).

♦ The validity of the strategy (A practical, step-by-step plan makes it easier for people to visualize what is not yet a reality. It also gives them a sense of how seriously you are taking the matter. If you don't take it very seriously, don't expect others to).

♦ The importance of this change (Change is hard, but in the long run, the consequences of not changing are harder).

For a ministry to continue to be successful and effective year after year, some things must change, and some things cannot be allowed to change. The wise leader knows the difference between the two. In a healthy organization the core values are unchangeably set in stone, but the strategies and programs to live those values out are changing constantly to adapt to the ongoing changes in the culture at large. Such an organization's life is a direct result of those abiding values and adapting strategies. In a dead or dying organization, the core values are changed by microscopic erosion. Unless vision continues to be cast, the "why" for starting things is replaced by the "what" of tradition. "We've always done it," becomes the driving motivation. Without the "why" you lose the most important tool in evaluating effectiveness. It is the only thing that tells you change is necessary, and without it, change becomes the enemy of the comfortable. If you find yourself trying to start something new in such an organization, before you can change anything you will first have to persuade all who are comfortable with status quo that they shouldn't be.

People will be convinced of the need for change...

♦ By your clarity in making the vision understandable—you must "put the cookies on the bottom shelf"

♦ By allowing the decision to be a process, not a point (you didn't arrive at your conclusions in one sitting, don't expect them to either)

♦ By your passion—as Howard Hendricks used to say, "If you want your people to bleed, you are going to have to hemorrhage!

♦ By your confidence in having heard from God—unless you are incredibly famous and talented, or intensely popular, your personal "Because I think we ought to" is probably not enough ethos to convince others to join in. If they can see that God is initiating this new venture, rather than you coming up with an idea and asking Him to bless it, He becomes the motivating factor.

♦ By God's Word and working—Depend on God, not self. This battle is won by prayer, not persuasion. Defend with Scripture, not just logic – God's Word changes opinions into convictions if the people want to follow God.

PHILOSOPHY OF BEGINNING A NEW MINISTRY (CONTINUED)

Let me interject an important side note here. Depending on where the people are, you may have to add a step to your process. If looking to Scripture for the model of how to run the church or ministry is not standard operating procedure, then this will have to be addressed. It is ineffective to defend change with Scripture if that is not what has normally been done in the past. You may have to take the time to establish Scripture as the authority before you use it to define direction.

2. Call for Commitment

Once you have cast vision for the new ministry, you will need to call for commitment. It takes people for ministry to happen. Some people naturally take the initiative to serve, but many don't unless they are invited to do so. Some don't think seriously about an opportunity to serve or be involved unless they are challenged to do so. Ask people to make a commitment to join in this venture. How you challenge is as important as that you challenge. Here are some suggestions…

♦ Don't ask too much too fast – make sure you help them to see that they can do what you are asking

♦ Don't ask for too little – small visions don't capture people

♦ Don't ask too generally – remember, everyone's challenge is no one's challenge

♦ Don't ask them to sign the rest of their life away (yet). Define a clear timeframe to the initial commitment you ask of them. Make the initial time commitment short enough to be reasonable (and easy if the larger vision is a hard sell). Make sure that in that initial stage you are giving them a taste of seeing God work.

♦ Don't ask them do anything you don't first equip them to do (and give them assurance you will do this).

3. Get Your Team Ready

A restaurant wouldn't dare open their doors for business without enough staff, or with an untrained or even under-trained staff. A good restaurateur knows that if you don't give that new customer a positive experience the first time, you may not get a second chance. Arrange the training and resources you think will be necessary to succeed. You must balance this preparation with faith. If you don't need God's help something is wrong. You must include faith in your preparation, but faith is no substitute for preparation. Stay sensitive to the Lord's leading as you move forward.

4. Start

Design your start strategically. Give some thought to the natural calendar of people's lives (e.g. mid-summer is not a natural time to start something new – September and January are). Look at the church calendar – don't try to compete with other major events that will conflict for people's attention. Consider how other events might keep people out. Consider how promotion for other events might drown your message out. You build steam riding a bicycle if you push on the different pedals in a coordinated fashion. Push a pedal at the wrong time and you hinder your progress instead of helping it. Follow a "cycles of momentum" strategy that fits in with the other pushes going on.

PHILOSOPHY OF BEGINNING A NEW MINISTRY (CONTINUED)

5. Invite the masses

Get the word out about what your ministry is designed to accomplish. I think this is where we must be careful though. We want to inform people, and even explain why they ought to be motivated, but we should not see it as our job to motivate them. That may sound strange at first but let me explain. We want to do all we can to make sure everyone knows about this ministry, but if we make it our job to talk people into it, we may not be leaving room for the Spirit to lead them. People who are talked into something by people can be talked out of it just as easily. When people are talked into something by God, He becomes the only one who can talk them out of it. Allow God to work in their hearts, and don't get in the way by using pressure tactics like guilt or manipulation or emotional appeals. Trust what He does instead of only what you do.

6. Filter the interested

No matter what your ministry is about, you need some way to filter out the folks you want to impact. Perhaps it is to identify those who have the greatest interest, or maybe the greatest need. However, you do it, you will need to design a strategy of response that helps you filter out the ones to focus on. How many people your new ministry can handle tells you how tight to make your filter – if you can only handle a few, set the standards higher with your first group.

7. Follow up on the interest

Take them a step further. If your ministry idea is legitimate, God will bring people who need it. When you meet a need, you always have an audience. If you apply the principles of God's truth to your ministry, then the unchurched open up to the idea that perhaps God's Word applies to all of their life as well. Make sure you put the bulk of your time, energy, and resources on moving with the interested instead of motivating those who aren't. If you minister, the people you affect become the greatest advertisement to others. Never sacrifice those who do come because of too much focus on those who don't.

8. Repeat the cycle

Reenlist those who committed to take part initially and ask for a longer and/or greater commitment. Some you may not want to reenlist to the same task for whatever reason. Don't feel obligated to keep someone in a position if it isn't working. Don't make them feel obligated to stay if they aren't motivated – whatever you have to do to get them to stay, you will have to keep doing to keep them there. Let God hire and fire – it is His job to send forth laborers in the harvest. Your job is to ask Him for laborers (prayer & faith), and to make the most of the laborers He sends (develop them, not just the ministry). People want to serve where they can see that they make a difference. They also want to serve where they are growing in the process as well.

If someone isn't working out…
Make sure they are equipped to do what you have asked. If more equipping is needed, give it (don't ever let busyness keep you from training. If you are too busy to train others, you will always be too busy because you'll be doing it without others). If the role isn't a good fit, look for another role in the task that is a better fit for them – never kick someone out of your ministry who wants to be in it (exception: those who aren't walking with God). Create a role for them to serve as they can if one doesn't currently exist. Involve the newcomers in helping you repeat the cycle (if you do this successfully and strategically, you ought to be able to handle more people with each cycle, and/or get the cycle going elsewhere).

SERVANT APPROACH LEADERSHIP TRAINING: Building Biblical Philosophy

Philosophy of Beginning a New Ministry (Continued)

8. Delegate and multiply

♦ Don't keep doing what others are ready to do (even if you like it – instead, find another place for yourself. Work yourself out of a job and you can move on to the next one God has for you, while allowing the total ministry to grow.

♦ Don't keep others from moving toward doing more (make sure your system allows them to become more involved).

♦ Don't limit your vision to one location – if you have a surplus of manpower it is time to expand.

Remember, there are a lot more who know how to minister TO people than there are who know how to minister THROUGH people. That skill is what separates leaders from the rest.

Conclusion:

What does it take to facilitate the birth of a new ministry? We must remind ourselves that the church is an organism, not an organization. If it is a healthy organism, new births should be a regular occurrence. It should be recognized that the impetus for starting a new ministry is not solely with the paid staff. A church should applaud creativity and enable the staff to begin new works, but a healthy church unleashes the laity to initiate ministry as well. Those in charge aren't always going to be the first to see the need or opportunity. They must be involved in that process though. Ministries that start without the blessing, involvement, and ownership of the church staff will never be woven into the life of the church as a whole. Not only will they lack the objective accountability that comes from being under authority, but they will also be deprived of the resourcing and helpful guidance they could have. Birthing a child only happens in a healthy way in the context of love, accountability, and commitment that marks a family. The same is true for birthing new ministries. I am always wary of the lone rangers who want to do their own thing and answer to only themselves.

Are you ready to start? The church is ready for your ministry!

Philosophy of Beginning a New Ministry (Continued)

Notes:

Philosophy of Biblical Counseling

© Copyright 1998, 2005 by Eddie Rasnake
You may reproduce this chapter at no charge as long as proper credit is given and no changes are made to the document.

Introduction

At a conference a number of years ago a very prominent figure in Christian counseling stated that he would not send his family or friends to a "Christian" counselor unless he knew that person's position on sin and the person of Christ. When someone influential within Christian counseling ministries warns that not all counseling under the Christian umbrella is decidedly Christian, it sends a significant message. It underscores the need to define exactly what is and is not Biblical counseling. Just because the counselor calls himself a Christian, it is no guarantee that his counseling is Biblical or offers Christ as the solution. A counselor's position on sin and the person of Christ may begin to clarify where they are coming from, but that alone is not enough to qualify their counseling as Christian or Biblical. We must also ask of the counselor's position on a number of other important issues. I would want to know what they believe about law and grace and the cross, about the sufficiency of the Word of God, and on the roles of humanistic Psychology, the counselor, and the Spirit of God in the counseling process.

What is "Christian" Counseling?

In defining "Christian" counseling, quite obviously we must separate out secular counseling by non-believers. There are really four camps of secular counseling: Psychoanalysis, Behavior Modification, Insight Therapy, and Transpersonal counseling. Psychoanalysis is rooted in the works of Freud involved with transactional analysis and cognitive therapies. Behavior Modification builds on the research of Watson and Skinner and their successors who concluded that man is merely a product of his environment. The focus is on changing a person from the outside in. The problem of such a view as it relates to sin is this—if man is merely the product of his environment, then he is not to blame for his sinful choices. It is his environment that is to blame for any maladjustment. Phenomenological or Insight Therapy, based on the work of Rogers, concludes that man has the solutions to his problems inside himself, and the role of the counselor is not to provide solutions but to assist the counselee in finding his own solutions. This is accomplished by "mirroring" or rephrasing the counselee's observations so that he or she can see what they are saying and discover their solution. One can easily see that if indeed the solution to his problems is within himself, he has no need for a savior. Perhaps this approach would work if sin had not left its stain on us. The fourth branch, Transpersonal counseling, utilizes parapsychology and occult phenomena to help someone cope with their circumstances. This often involves "channeling" or communicating with dead spirits through a medium. Influences of this type of counseling come from Transcendental Meditation, Edgar Cayce, EST, and a host of Eastern religious beliefs in western packaging that all fall under the umbrella of the New Age movement.

Although Christian counseling is generally separated from purely secular therapy, there is much spill over. Often the Christian counselor has gone through much secular training. Without a strong grid of Scripture and a confidence in it, there is a tendency to allow secular philosophies and approaches to seep into a counselor's thinking and approach. It is important at this point to acknowledge that being secular does not automatically mean that a perspective is false. Many Biblical truths are adapted to secular audiences. In addition, our view of the nature of truth must be examined. I believe that the Holy Bible is wholly true. It contains no error. I do not, however, believe that the Bible contains all truth. What I consider essential is that all propositions of truth must be held up against God's revelation. A perspective cannot be taken as true if it directly contradicts what God has said.

Philosophy of Biblical Counseling (Continued)

Modern Christian counseling exhibits two dominant approaches: Psychological and Theological. The Psychological approach to Christian counseling draws on the secular work of Psychology and redefines it in Christian terms. There also exists a Theological vein of Christian counseling. It is based not in applying the tenets of secular Psychology, but in applying the Word of God. While we may be tempted to try and fit all counselors into one box or the other, individual counselors who operate completely in one box or the other are rare. Contemporary Christian counseling can better be viewed as a spectrum. Most counselors would fit somewhere between the two approaches, but at some point in the process they are forced to choose one over the other. The two are not compatible enough to stay blended.

The major divisions of Psychology-based Christian counseling are Analytic/cognitive (dealing primarily with the mind), Gestalt (dealing primarily with the emotions), Rational/emotive (blending the two), Behavioral (dealing with changing how we perform, not how we think and feel), Insight therapies, and Eclectic counseling (basically, whatever works). These disciplines are often steeped in Christian terminology and generally are administered by those who call themselves believers. They are, however, decidedly secular in their view of humanity and in their practical approach. Because of this, the therapies operate on the level of the flesh rather than the spirit. They either succeed or fail in their attempts to strengthen the flesh. If any change occurs on the level of the spirit, it is purely accidental and independent of the counseling process. A person who seeks out this kind of Christian counseling can expect care, not cure. Research indicates that with certain problems the success rate of a person conquering that issue is the same with or without counseling. The primary benefit with such should be credited to time and the gaining of life wisdom, rather than counseling sessions.

Theological counseling must also be subdivided. Of those who see the primary agent in counseling as Scripture, there are two approaches: Law and Grace. Theological counseling which focuses on law emphasizes doing in order to be. Their trumpet call is obedience as they try to move people toward applying the principles of Scripture. While often correct in trying to deal with the wrong thinking behind wrong behavior, their approach offers little comfort to damaged emotions, and does not emphasize the necessity of the work of Christ in facilitating obedience. Instead of the internal working of the Spirit of God, quite often change is brought about as behavior is modified through accountability and peer pressure without bringing about real change in the inner person. Grace counseling, in contrast to law-focused counseling, emphasizes being in order to do. In other words, it is correcting our relationship to God that is central, and once this is done, behavior will move in the right direction. While obedience is still important in grace counseling, it is not the focus. Rather, the focus is on surrender to the Lord's control that results in obedience. Instead of placing the emphasis on applying Scriptural principles, grace counseling emphasizes a mind-renewed life that is being transformed by the Spirit of God. Law focuses on getting flesh to "tow-the-line," while grace focuses on recognizing that flesh cannot please God. Therefore, in grace-based counseling, the central solution to all mental and emotional problems (except of course those that are physical and physically treatable) is yielding our lives to the control of Christ: letting Jesus be Jesus in us.

What Is the *REAL* Problem?

The impetus for someone seeking out Biblical counseling is invariably some manifestation of behavioral or emotional problems. Unfortunately, most so-called Christian counseling treats the individual as if the abnormal emotions or behaviors are the problem, when in fact they are the symptoms of the problem. The innate problem of a human is not that they sin, but that they are a sinner in need of a savior. Consider this analogy. When you come home and discover your basement is flooded because a pipe has burst, it would be ludicrous to suggest that you could resolve the dilemma with a bucket and mop. The flooded basement

Philosophy of Biblical Counseling (Continued)

is not the real problem; it is the result of the real problem. The real problem is the break in the pipe, and until that is repaired, you really haven't made any progress. Mopping may give you the satisfaction of feeling like you are at least doing something, but in fact, all your activity results in no productivity. What you are doing is accomplishing nothing of real consequence to the fundamental problem. In the same way, counseling that focuses on changing destructive behaviors and attitudes, instead of first dealing with correcting our relationship with God, is futile. While this approach may make it easier to cope with the problem, it will never cure it.

In this counseling analogy, fixing the broken pipe is figurative of returning to a position of total surrender, and mopping up the mess is figurative of addressing the behaviors and attitudes that need correcting. Once the figurative pipe is repaired, there is still mopping to be done. Sometimes it is necessary to remove some of the water before you can get to the real problem. We must never lose sight of the ultimate objective—to deal with the root problem instead of the symptoms. One of the blessings of spiritual life is that quite often, once the figurative pipe is repaired and a right relationship with God is reestablished, many of the behaviors and attitudes that were so in need of change take care of themselves. Those that are not remedied by going to the cross, God intends to deal with through growth. In other words, some of the problems of the soul go away and some grow away. That is where discipleship must be viewed as part of the solution. Once the victory of the cross becomes a reality, dealing with the symptoms is mostly a "mop-up" operation. This is not to say that the issues that have troubled a person are overlooked, but they are dealt with from the vantage point of having gained victory—not in an attempt to work toward victory. It is a given that some who seek help have an organic problem that must be treated by the medical profession. If we do not believe it wrong to add insulin to a body that produces too little, we should not have a problem with hormone replacement or the treatment of chemical imbalances. A word of perspective is warranted here. It should be recognized that wrong behavior produces consequences in the body. While some believe that a chemical imbalance causes wrong behavior, the reality of sin's consequences makes it necessary to consider that perhaps it is wrong behavior which produces a chemical imbalance. While it may be necessary to treat such an imbalance medically, unless the wrong behavior is dealt with in a Biblical manner, the medication will not resolve the problem. As an additional consideration, some counselees are not dealing with reality and cannot be ministered to in an outpatient setting. However, these are in the decided minority. Most counseling needs could, and should, be met by the ministry of the local church.

An important distinction must be made when we speak of a need for "counseling." There is inherent danger in this perspective. We can subtly communicate that there is only one problem and once that is taken care of, the person is fine. In reality, we will never "arrive" this side of heaven, and there will always be a need for growth. While one-to-one counseling may be necessary to correct blockages and put a person back on the right path, once there, change and growth are still needed. The advantage of the term "discipleship" is that it correctly communicates this truth—I will always have room for more growth. In Philippians 3:12 Paul writes: "*...not that I have already obtained it or have become perfect, but I press on...*". He was speaking of spiritual conformity to Christ, and remarkably, he had been walking with Christ for 25-30 years when he wrote those words. He had still not arrived, nor have we. This reality must always be communicated.

Who is the "Therapist?"

Traditional Christian counseling involves two parties: the counselee and the therapist. But this is not a true, Biblical view. In Biblical counseling, the therapist is the Spirit of God applying the Word of God to

Philosophy of Biblical Counseling (Continued)

the heart of the individual. The counselor is a facilitator, but the active agents are the Spirit and the Word. If change is wrought, there is where the credit lies. If this is not understood, counseling can facilitate a dependence on the counselor instead of what is really needed: a greater dependence on Christ who is our life. The beauty of the Holy Spirit as therapist is that because He is omniscient, omnipotent, and omnipresent, He requires much less time to transform a life than is generally consumed in the traditional approach to therapy. After all, He is the *Wonderful Counselor*. While therapy is not to be disdained as being of the devil, it would more appropriately be called *care* rather than *cure*. And to be fair, there are many more hurting people who would opt for care than cure. This is not to say that a person receives no help with a problem in therapy. Many have found much better adjustment psychologically in traditional approaches to therapy. However, unless God is allowed to work in the heart, it will be found that the self-life has been strengthened in the process. If it is accepted that self-centeredness or flesh is the root problem, then it becomes obvious that *care* has rendered *cure* a setback.

Because of this reality, the counselor must keep the goal in focus, and must develop discernment in assessing if the Spirit has prepared the heart for doing business with God. If so, his responsibility is to lead the individual to the cross so that they can die to themselves and yield every area of their lives to Christ. If they are not at that point, then the counselor needs to focus on teaching them the whole counsel of God about the necessity of surrender. It must be recognized that the symptoms which motivated the individual to seek counseling may be the very agent of God designed to bring them to the end of themselves. If we merely treat the symptoms, we may take the pressure off and help them to cope, actually delaying the work of God through their circumstances. God is always working on our character, molding us to be like Christ, and He is always calling us to surrender. The counselor must make certain he is working with the Lord and not against Him.

Is the Word of God Really Sufficient?

Defining the place and approach of counseling in the church is first and foremost, a debate about the efficacy of the Word of God. Is the Word and work of God in our life really enough to solve the problems and consequences of sin? Many today by their actions exemplify a belief that the Bible and a pastor may be helpful in dealing with minor problems, but for major difficulties something else is needed. They look to the "professionals," many of whom may be Christians, but more often than not, rely on secular training and methods. There is a fundamental question that we must answer. Are God and His Word enough?

📖 Read 2 Peter 1:2-4 and write what you learn there about how God desires to deal with sin and its consequences in our lives.

A German dramatist described his relationship to the Word of God like this: "I have read many books, but the Bible stands alone - it reads me." In 2 Timothy, the last letter Paul wrote before his death, he gives a series of important admonitions to Timothy, his son in the faith and the principal leader of the church at Ephesus. You might call this book of the Bible, Paul's spiritual "last will and testament." Look at 2 Timothy 3:16-17 and answer the questions below.

In verse 16 what are the four things Scripture is "*profitable*" for and what do you think they mean?

PHILOSOPHY OF BIBLICAL COUNSELING (CONTINUED)

Look at verse 17 and identify what it is that equips the man of God for "*every good work*."

📖 Use the chart below: look up the verses and record what they teach about the *nature of the Word* in the center column and the *benefits of the Word* in the rightmost column. Not every verse will have something for both columns. This study gives us a practical sense of what the Word of God is able to do in one's life.

Passage	Nature of the Word	Benefits of the Word
Psalm 19:7a		
Psalm 19:7b		
Psalm 19:8a		
Psalm 19:8b		
Psalm 19:9a		
Psalm 19:9b		
Psalm 19:10		
Psalm 19:11		
Psalm 19:12		
Psalm 19:13		
Psalm 19:14		

PHILOSOPHY OF BIBLICAL COUNSELING (CONTINUED)

Christian Counseling Versus Christ-life Counseling

As we have seen, not all counseling that calls itself "Christian" really recognizes the truth that victory is only found when Christ is my life; that is to say, control of my life is yielded to Him, and self is no longer dominating the life. But how does this reality of the "Christ-life" manifest itself, and what must be the perspective of the counselor? Christ-life counseling differs because what the counselor believes about the problem and its cure is different. The Christ-life counselor has a different view of sin, of Christ and how He relates to the believer, of the cross, of grace, and even of the problems of the counselee.

WHAT MUST THE COUNSELOR BELIEVE ABOUT SIN?

Is it something that will dominate us for the rest of our lives? If this is the counselor's view, they will most likely attempt to bring comfort to defeated believers. These defeated ones will be reinforced in their attempts to cope with failure, instead of the Biblical reality that we can experience victory over sin. Second Corinthians 2:14 teaches: *"But thanks be to God, who always leads us in triumph in Christ."* If we are not walking toward victory, then we are not following where God is leading. Romans 6:6 promises that we should no longer be slaves to sin.

WHAT MUST THE COUNSELOR BELIEVE ABOUT CHRIST AND HOW HE RELATES TO THE BELIEVER?

Is Christ merely someone to imitate? Many Christian counselors prescribe that the defeated believer should read more about Jesus and try harder to follow His example. This advice is destined for failure because one of two things must happen. Possibly, the defeated believer will improve his or her behavior; and this will lead to pride, self-righteousness, and self-dependence. On the other hand, probably the defeated believer will fail to permanently improve their behavior; and this will lead to guilt and the feeling that one might as well give up. The life that fluctuates between guilt and pride is not the "overwhelmingly conquering" we are promised in Romans 8. The Christian life is not me trying to be like Jesus. If I could be like Jesus by trying harder, then I don't need a Savior. He didn't need to die on the cross. The Christian life is taking God at His word (that I have the very life of Jesus in me to empower me) and appropriating that truth by faith.

WHAT MUST THE COUNSELOR BELIEVE ABOUT THE CROSS?

Is it only the place where Jesus died for my sins? Yes, praise God, our sins were forgiven by the work of Christ on the cross, but this is only half the message of the cross. Not only is the cross the place where Christ died, but it is also the place where I die. I must die daily to self-living, or I cannot experience the new life of the resurrection. When I die, Christ becomes my life. At the cross I receive a new past. I am no longer a slave to my old past, but I exchange it for Christ who has a past of victory. My present becomes His present. His victory becomes mine and His future glory as well. There is freedom at the cross, but to experience it, I must die. I died positionally when I first trusted Christ, and I die experientially when I surrender control of my life to Him moment by moment.

WHAT MUST THE COUNSELOR BELIEVE ABOUT GRACE?

Is grace merely the overlooking of my shortcomings? While it certainly is that it is much more. Grace is not only the freedom to not be perfect, but it is also the empowerment to become perfect. Grace not only frees me from the penalty of ungodliness and unrighteousness, but it instructs me toward righteousness (Titus 2:11-13), and it enables me to become what I am not. As I yield my life to Christ, He literally lives His life through me. Removal of the guilt of sin is not as wonderful as the replacement of the guilty. There is no hopelessness for those who are in Christ. This is truly amazing grace.

PHILOSOPHY OF BIBLICAL COUNSELING (CONTINUED)

WHAT DOES THE COUNSELOR BELIEVE ABOUT THE REAL PROBLEMS OF THE COUNSELEE?

Is the counselee's problem his or her circumstances or relationship with God? Is the problem their past, or that they is not exchanging their past for Christ's? Is the problem that a person can't please God, or that one has failed to recognize that only Christ can? Is the problem that of failing in one's identity as mate/parent/worker etc., or of finding one's identity in relationships or performance instead of in Christ? Is the problem that the person is not accepted, or that he or she doesn't understand or live in the reality that they are accepted in the Beloved? Is the problem that self is not able to do what it should, or is the real problem in believing that self could apart from Christ? Galatians 2:21 says, *"I do not nullify the grace of God; for if righteousness comes through the Law, then Christ died needlessly."* To paraphrase, if my marriage problems could be cured by my own effort (law) then Christ died in vain. If my drug addiction could be cured by my own effort (law) then Christ died in vain. If my sexual lusts could be cured by my own effort (law) then Christ died in vain. If my emotional problems could be cured by my own effort (law) then Christ died in vain. This is not to say that psychological care may not help me cope with these problems (sins), but that only the grace of God expressed through the indwelling power of Christ can merit God's declaration of righteousness. We know that the new birth came by a gift of the Spirit, but do we know that our maturity is also a matter of trusting and not a matter of trying harder? Galatians 3:3, *"Are you so foolish? Having begun by the Spirit, are you now being perfected by the flesh?"*

Counseling as Equipping

What is the place of counseling in the life and ministry of the church? If we understand counseling as trying to help failing Christians cope with their failure, then we will never place this ministry as an integral part of the church. But if we rightly understand that true counseling is communicating the Christ-life, then counseling is no longer burdensome because we know where we are going, and we know how to get there: by the way of the cross. Counseling seen this way is rightly viewed as equipping, for no one can minister effectively until they have been to the cross. When we begin to see counseling as equipping, it becomes as important as our group teaching ministries, and we will begin to utilize our manpower and resources accordingly. When we recognize that the ultimate goal of counseling rightly done is to communicate the Christ-life, then we no longer limit it to the paid professionals. Instead, we equip and unleash the laity to help shoulder the task. As our counselee's experience the cross, they are moved a long way toward being able to communicate it to others. This is ministry as it should be. The work of the church is for the leadership God raises up to rightly fulfill their role in *"the equipping of the saints for the work of service, to the building up of the body of Christ"* (Ephesians 4:12).

PHILOSOPHY OF BIBLICAL COUNSELING (CONTINUED)

Notes:

Philosophy of Children's Ministry

© Copyright 2005 by Eddie Rasnake
You may reproduce this chapter at no charge as long as proper credit is given and no changes are made to the document.

The State of Children Today

How important are children in the ministry? ...in society? ...at home? How important are they to God? These questions are more than rhetorical. I can't imagine anyone giving a verbal "no" to any of those questions, but the actions of society as well as the church often send a mixed message. Much money, manpower, and resources are often directed there. Yet sometimes the spiritual input is lacking, and the practical function is more like childcare than discipleship. The actions of society seem to send a message of insignificance and low expectations. George Barna's book, <u>Transforming Children Into Spiritual Champions</u>, capped 2 1/2 years of research on the state of children and children's ministry. Let's look at some of the results of his research of children in today's society.

- One out of every three children born in the U.S. each year is born to an unmarried woman.
- According to the Center for Disease Control (CDC), almost one out of every ten teenagers had sexual intercourse prior to his or her thirteenth birthday, and that number is steadily rising.
- One out of every four children presently lives with a single parent, and about half find themselves in that situation before they reach their 18th birthday.
- Kids ages 2 to 7 average nearly 25 hours per week of mass media intake; the figure balloons to almost 48 hours each week among those aged 8 to 13.
- About one out of every ten 8th graders smokes daily; one out of four by the age of 17. One out of five used drugs of some type in the past year; one out of three were drunk at least once in the past year.
- 44% of all preteens admit that they don't have any role models.
- When children are asked to identify the three most important people in the world to them, only one-third name their mother or father.
- Two-thirds of all adolescents are booked into a full slate of activities.
- 45% of elementary schools reported one or more incidents of violent crime. 74% of middle schools reported one or more incidents of violent crime.
- About 7% of children between the ages of 6 and 11 have been diagnosed with attention deficit hyperactivity disorder (ADHD). Millions of them are treated with Ritalin, antidepressants and other psychiatric drugs.

In many homes, children hear that they matter, but see that they don't in the lack of time and attention directed their way. There is no question that children are the "biggest losers" in our present *me first* society. George Barna tells us that "...relatively few youngsters will be physically abandoned by their parents, but millions will be traumatized by receiving their parents' emotional leftovers, as well as by the divorce, separation, and adulterous activities that will shatter their family unity" (<u>Transforming Children Into Spiritual Champions</u>). It does seem that more children are having to rear themselves than ever before. Some time ago one of my sons had a friend from school over. In the course of their play, I joined them for a game of Mario Kart on the Nintendo Game Cube. I was surprised at what a big deal that seemed to our guest. In the course of conversation, he related "My dad would never do this—he is too busy." The boy didn't say this with any malice or even hurt. To him it was a simple matter-of-fact. Maybe my home is more unusual than I realize. It does seem more children are having to raise themselves than ever before. While parents and society and even the church may sometimes make children less a priority than they should be.

PHILOSOPHY OF CHILDREN'S MINISTRY (CONTINUED)

God's View of Children
The disturbing statistics regarding children in today's society are not what God had in mind when he commanded Adam and Eve to *"be fruitful and multiply the earth"*. As seen throughout Scripture, children are precious to God. Look up the following passages and write down what God says about children.

- Gen. 33:5—

- Psalm 127:3—

- Psalm 127:5—

- Exodus 22:22-24—

- Proverbs 17:6—

- Psalm 78:4-6—

Wow! In the eyes of God, children are our future kings and princes...in the eyes of the world, children are rugrats. In God's eyes, children are a means of God's grace...in the eyes of the world, children are a detriment to our means. In God's eyes, children are rewards...in the eyes of the world, children are regrets. In the eyes of God, children are a blessing...in the eyes of the world, children are a burden. In the eyes of God, children are crowns to the aged...in the eyes of the world, children cramp our style. In God's eyes, children represent the largest unreached people group in the world...in today's real world, children are the largest neglected people group. Ministry to children both at home and at church must reflect God's view of children. While parents and society and even the church may sometimes make children less a priority than they should be, this was not the case in Jesus' earthly ministry.

  Read Matthew 18:1-10—What question started this conversation?

What is the main point Jesus is making in setting a child as an example to this adult audience in Matthew 18:3-4?

What child-like attributes does Jesus applaud here?

Look up the word *"receive"* in Matthew 18:5 and record your thoughts on the light this meaning sheds on understanding this verse.

What consequences does Jesus say are warranted for those who cause children to stumble (18:6-7)?

Considering Matthew 18:10, what do you think constitutes to *"despise"* little ones, and how does that compare to what the verse reveals of God's attitude?

SERVANT APPROACH LEADERSHIP TRAINING: Building Biblical Philosophy   (revised 2/20/223)

PHILOSOPHY OF CHILDREN'S MINISTRY (CONTINUED)

Consider the point he made in Matthew 18. Jesus set a child as the example for adults to follow. He applauded the child's humility and trust and gave that as the model of the heart God wants. He went on to address the importance of how we treat children. Matthew 18:5 suggests that our attitude toward children says much about our attitude toward God. Conversely, the passage continues with warnings of how serious a matter it is to cause a child to stumble. Jesus considered being drown with a millstone tied to your neck as not strong enough consequence for such a crime. This perspective Jesus taught must be set in our minds against the insignificant and de-emphasized role of children in Palestinian society.

Jesus summarized His instruction about children in Matthew 18:10 by saying, *"See that you do not despise one of these little ones, for I say to you that their angels in heaven continually see the face of My Father who is in heaven."* Think about the implications of this verse. Consider what it says about how important children are to God. Apparently, children have guardian angels (see also Psalm 91:11 and Acts 12:15) who report directly to God (who *"constantly behold the face of My Father…"*). That sends a pretty clear message that children matter greatly to God. But think about Jesus' admonition here. He uses an imperative (command) rather than a suggestion, and charges us to see that we do not *"despise"* these little ones. The English term suggests hate, and with that understanding most of us would let ourselves off the hook as being not guilty. But the Greek word (*kataphroneo*) literally means "to think down on." It can mean contempt or to think lightly of something—to not take it seriously. Whoa! It is a little harder to acquit ourselves of that. If we as individuals—or as the church—do not take seriously the needs of children, or the incredible impact on the world we could potentially have by impacting them, then we have need of repentance.

📖 Read John 6:1-9 in its context and contrast what Jesus did with the boy's lunch with how it was viewed by the disciples.

You may not have remembered this, but when Jesus fed the 5,000 it was a child who shared his lunch to help meet the need (John 6:9). Some of the details are sketchy, but a few things are clear. The boy had enough food to share, and this was made known to the disciples. It implies that perhaps the boy offered his food and was rebuffed by the disciples. Notice verse 6 indicates this circumstance was a test for the disciples. God can make much of little. That is true of lunches as well as little children. In my experience, it seems children are more spiritually open and hungry than adults as a whole. Why put so much of our energy sowing seed on hard soil when theirs is so soft?

Take a moment and write down any reasons that come to mind for why we can think lightly of children.

📖 Look up 1 Corinthians 13:11 and write what you learn about children from this verse.

There is a clear message here for adults who would minister to children—they don't think the same way you do! If we are to minister effectively to children, we must do what Jesus did with us. He left heaven and got down on the level of His audience. He was Spirit, not human, but He became human so that we might understand. He *"dwelt among us."* The intellectual development of children is a work in progress.

SERVANT APPROACH LEADERSHIP TRAINING: Building Biblical Philosophy

PHILOSOPHY OF CHILDREN'S MINISTRY (CONTINUED)

Paul states here, *"When I was a child, I used to speak like a child, think like a child, reason like a child; when I became a man, I did away with childish things."* One of the reasons children get bored with church is because it is often boring—especially to them. Little is aimed at keeping their attention. This is a crime. In a world where church competes with X-Box and Disney for the attention of children, shame on us for our unwillingness to break free (even a little) from flannelgraph Jesus. Many say that children need to be taught how to sit still and listen. Howard Hendricks, however, offers this perspective in his outstanding instruction to teachers: *The Seven Laws of the Teacher*. "Every time you tell that child to sit still, the Holy Spirit is telling him to wiggle!" I really do believe that we often work against God instead of with Him when it comes to church. Oh sure, we will arrange Sunday School for children, but the church service goes way over their heads. Come to think of it, they may not be the only target we are missing. It is well and good to teach a child respect and manners, but don't try to make them not be a child! Children ought to be made to feel comfortable in church, not uncomfortable. That they are so neglected in the average worship service says to me that many churches do fulfill the definition of *"despise"* that Jesus commanded against.

📖 Read Proverbs 22:15 and Proverbs 13:20, and then connect the two thoughts.

Proverbs 22:15 tells us *"Foolishness is bound up in the heart of a child"*. In Proverbs 13:20 we learn that *"…the companion of fools will suffer harm"*. As we relate these two verses to children's ministry, we see that in the area of socialization the great need of a child is not interaction with children his own age (who also have foolishness bound up in their hearts), but interaction with adults to learn their wisdom. Therefore, focused attention from adult instructors is essential. To facilitate this the teacher/pupil ratio should be monitored closely. It is also desirable that both men and women are represented to the children. If there are no men represented in your children's ministry, that sends a silent message to all those kids.

As we look at curriculum, obviously, we desire strong input from the Scriptures, but we must be careful not to fall prey to the worldly philosophy that more is always better. We will have a far greater impact in the long run if we do a more thorough job teaching fewer truths. Each lesson should have only one major point with all the morning's activities (crafts, music, stories, etc.) centered around that theme. When God's truth is presented in a fun and creative way, more of it sticks with the child. He or she will want to come back for more. Not only that, but they'll want to bring a friend next time. That is huge! That's when Sunday School becomes outreach, when we showcase the truths of God as so attractive, it leaves children craving more.

Another essential element to curriculum selection is how it communicates its truth. Hebrews 13:9 teaches us that grace strengthens the heart and any other teaching is *"varied and strange teaching"* by which the hearer is *"carried away"* or put off track. One of the greatest heresies of our day is legalism and there should be given no leeway to this in teaching our precious little ones. We would do well to remind ourselves of Christ's admonition in Matthew 18 that it would be better to have a millstone around our neck and be cast in the sea than to cause a little one to stumble. As James warns us (James 3:1), teachers will incur a stricter judgment.

Philosophy of Children's Ministry (Continued)

📖 Take a few moments to consider 1 Peter 2:2 along with 1 Corinthians 3:2 and relate what you learn there.

A final concept worth considering is mentioned in 1 Peter 2:2 and 1 Corinthians 3:2. Here in 1 Peter we find that a newborn babe (spiritually speaking) should be given milk (the pure milk of the Word) that he might grow in respect to salvation. It must not stay that way though. Paul tells us in 1 Corinthians that a believer should progress to be able to handle solid food. As we relate this to children's ministry, we see the need to pre-digest spiritual food so that the little ones can use it, but we must help them to grow in their ability to go deeper in the Word.

If these priorities are reflected in our children's ministry coupled with a trust in God rather than our plans and programs, we can expect to see good fruit.

Recommended resources:
- *Shepherding A Child's Heart* by Tedd Tripp...this is an excellent resource that helps parents and teachers look beyond a legalistic focus on actions and behavior modification, instead, directing their attention and energies on shepherding the hearts of children.
- *Firm Foundations: Creation to Christ* by Trevor McIlwain and Nancy Everson...this was originally written as an adult curriculum for tribal situations ministering to people with no Biblical foundation at all. The premise is that if we start our explanation of the gospel with Christ, they will fit Him in with all the other gods they believe in, but if we start with creation and work our way forward to Christ they will see His uniqueness and the fundamental need for a sacrifice. There is also a children's version, and the premise is certainly applicable to our approach to bringing children to a point of seeing their need for Jesus.

Children's Ministry and the Home

The responsibility of a child's spiritual instruction lies with the parents (Deuteronomy 6:6-9, 11:18-19) and must happen in the home. Spiritual life that is only exercised on Sunday will have little impact on a child growing in the Lord. This responsibility goes far beyond merely taking them to church and reading the Bible to them. The truths of God must first be embraced by the parents, then translated to the child. Considering this, it is to be the primary emphasis of our children's ministry to support the Biblical position of the home. The reality is that the average child is with mom and/or dad for 132 hours a week, at school for 35 hours a week, and at church for just a couple of hours each week. We see our investment as a supplement to, not a substitute for the parent's objective of raising godly children. As much as we want to help mom and dad, we also need mom and dad to help us. A dynamic partnership is crucial.

We believe that it is the responsibility and privilege of parents to establish the child in his relationship with Christ. We will serve the parents through teaching the children the gospel and at appropriate times giving opportunity for decision. As a child's spiritual interest is awakened and expressed it is essential that the teacher begin a dialogue with the parent.

SERVANT APPROACH LEADERSHIP TRAINING: Building Biblical Philosophy

PHILOSOPHY OF CHILDREN'S MINISTRY (CONTINUED)

The Objectives of our Children's Ministry

The structural framework of our Children's ministry will consist of programs, but these are not to be simply adopted from other places. Rather they are developed and adapted based on the principles of Scripture and the prompting of God's Spirit. Programs (the "hows") continually change but the principles (the "whys") never do. It is following the promptings of the Spirit that give us the creativity to tailor-make programs to meet specific needs. "We've always done it that way" is not sufficient reason for a program, nor is a past history of success. Our central focus must always be to follow the Lord Jesus.

The mission of our Children's ministry is: *Reaching the next generations by helping families introduce today's children to Jesus Christ and shepherd them to become kingdom seekers.* This will succeed as it is done in an atmosphere of love, acceptance, and encouragement working in tandem with accountability and challenge. Our Sunday morning activities are designed to communicate Biblical truth and foster godly character in the most effective ways for each developmental age group. Our evening programs are designed to support and enhance what happens on Sunday morning.

Nursery Level

In the nursery (birth to the third birthday) the children are for the most part non-verbal, non-cognitive communicators. Understanding this, we seek to communicate God's love through an environment that is safe, secure, soothing, and structured. This is to be accomplished through adequate staffing, organized and safeguarded registry, sanitary practices, appropriate lighting and background music, developmental toys, and focused attention. As children near two years old they are beginning to develop language skills allowing for the implementation of short, entertaining Bible stores and fun, active songs.

Pre-school Level

It is at the pre-school level that foundations for Biblical learning are laid in earnest. We seek to instill in our children first and foremost the central role of the Word of God in spiritual life, giving them a grasp of its authoritative and instructive nature. At this level we can accomplish our objectives through a) teaching basic Bible doctrines from the standpoint of God's character (e.g., God is holy, therefore He must judge sin, God is loving, therefore He gives grace and mercy through Christ to those who receive Him), b) modeling godly character through the examples of Old and New Testament personalities, and c) instructing toward godly living through parables and Bible stores. Simple application is designed relevant to this level and memorization of short Bible verses is introduced. Music is incorporated for variety and as a communication vehicle.

Levels K-3

In Grades K-3 children are beginning to learn to read. Their ability to communicate and understand allows for dealing with spiritual issues at a deeper, more meaningful level. Now they can begin to read the Bible for themselves so our curriculum and approach should function in a manner that encourages Bible discovery. The focus of our activities and instruction is to point toward the development of godly character and the application of Bible principles.

Middle Grades—4 and 5

At this level we begin to introduce the principles of worship and Biblical teaching as the children begin to participate in some worship services. The foundational process begun in pre-school and K-3 is intensified and broadened to incorporate becoming familiar with books of the Bible and key topical passages (e.g., 1 Corinthians 13, Gal. 5:22-23, etc.). Inductive Bible study is introduced and practiced, and the children are pointed toward an accurate handling of the Scriptures. By the time children graduate to youth, they should have a basic cross-section of the Christian life.

Philosophy of Children's Ministry (Continued)

Children's Ministry Core Values

- **To supplement the home**—Our objective is to help the parents succeed in raising godly children, not to be a substitute for their spiritual input. We see the home as the primary place, and the parents as the primary agents, for the child's spiritual growth.

- **To lay a foundation in the Child's Life**—We want to see to it that the children growing up through our ministry systematically work through the Scriptures so that a solid foundation is already in place when they reach the difficult years of puberty.

- **We are process-oriented, not event-oriented**—The focus of our Children's ministry is not on decisions for Christ, but the process of spiritual growth. We encourage decisions for Christ, and we encourage our leaders to be ready when God convicts a child, but our focus is to be on the process—working for the long haul.

- **We are child-centered, not adult-centered**—All teaching and programs must be relevant to the child and communicated on their level. We must enter their world and use their language. This affects facilities as well—rooms should be designed to be child-centered, and they should also be well equipped and supplied.

- **Appropriate blending of routine and creativity**—A young child has a high need for routines, but as he ages his Sunday school experience requires more and more creativity.

- **Our teaching is relevant to life**—The Biblical content is to be communicated in a manner that is relevant to their day-to-day living. The goal of Bible study is not simply information, but application.

- **We are relational, not informational**—A teacher's evaluation is not just "Did the information come across?" but "Did I come across?" Who we are communicates more than what we say.

- **Fun first—Banish Boredom**—We believe that if a child is having fun, they are most receptive to learn. We also believe it is a crime to bore people with the eternal riches of Christ.

- **Everything must be evaluated**—"Why are we doing it?" "What would work better?" should show up regularly in our conversations. We never do things because that is the way we have always done them. Scripture, not tradition, is our standard, and relevance is our goal.

- **Our message is Christ**—We will focus on the person of Christ and a personal relationship with Him, not simply morality and ethics.

Philosophy of Children's Ministry (Continued)

Notes:

Philosophy of Calling Church Staff

© Copyright 1998 Eddie Rasnake
You may reproduce this chapter at no charge as long as proper credit is given and no changes are made to the document.

Perhaps nothing is more intimidating to a group of people than bearing the responsibility of calling a senior or supporting pastor. The process is always long and complicated, and will be evaluated long after it is finished. Those entrusted with so great a task often are given no clear direction on how to accomplish it. Even when a process is established beforehand by others, the group, if they hold their role with integrity, must ask, "Is the process given to us the right one?" Fortunately, this assignment is not arbitrary or subjective. There are objective principles in the Word of God to guide such a process. Before we look at some of those principles, let's identify what not to do.

How Not To Do It

Most churches who are looking for a staff member start by forming a "Search Committee." Then they attempt to get many résumés and begin the daunting task of weeding through them to find the pot of gold at the end of the rainbow. Prospects are paraded before the church with their best foot forward as the field is narrowed. When the "most qualified" is identified, the committee makes its move. Hopefully, they can agree on one who hopefully still wants them. If the vacancy is successfully filled, we assume "mission accomplished," but was it? According to Southern Baptists, the average pastorate doesn't last four years—barely past the "honeymoon" (see *Southern Baptists Churches Today*, Phillip B. Jones, February 2001, www.namb.net, page V). Other denominations report similar difficulties. While pastors are leaving churches at a more rapid pace than ever, numerous studies have concluded that the most productive years for the pastor may depend on longevity. Lyle Schaller found that the greatest growth of churches occurred in years 5-8 of a pastor's tenure. Kirk Hadaway, whose research was limited to Southern Baptist pastors, concluded that the most productive years were 3-6. George Barna's data point to increasing productivity for pastors between years 3-15 (*Ten Tough Questions for Church Leaders, Part 2*, Thom Rainer, www.rainergroup.com/rainergroup/ 10questions_part2.asp). Could it be that we are using the wrong process? The résumé approach may successfully hire a sales person, but it is closer to the world than the Scriptures. I believe it turns the process into a beauty pageant with the biblical concept of "calling" shoved to the side. The focus centers on the person more than God. Every church I know has endured some messy mistakes. Maybe we get the wrong answer because we ask the wrong question – "Who is the most qualified?" instead of "Who is God calling?"

What is a "Calling"?

A specific concept emerges with Paul's self-description to the Romans: *"called as an apostle"* (Romans 1:1). The Greek word *kletos* can be used generally (e.g. "called" by God as believers). Sometimes however, it points to a specific calling and task. Paul told the Corinthians he was *"called as an apostle of Jesus Christ by the will of God"* (1 Corinthians 1:1). He was not self-appointed. The Sanhedrin search committee had quickly affirmed his chosen vocation as a persecutor of the church. The "called" concept though, speaks of God's selection. The human side of the task is not making our choice but discerning His choice and affirming that. Understanding this might have helped Korah. He argued others were just as qualified to lead as Moses. To use modern terminology, he was saying, "Our résumés are just as good as yours."

> 📖 Read the story of Korah's rebellion in Number 16 and identify Korah's arguments and how Moses defends himself against them.

SERVANT APPROACH LEADERSHIP TRAINING: Building Biblical Philosophy

Philosophy of Calling Church Staff (Continued)

Moses' only defense however said nothing of being "most qualified." His only credential was *"...the Lord has sent me to do all these deeds; for this is not my doing"* (Numbers 16:28). If we selected Jesus' disciples by résumés, I doubt any of the twelve *"uneducated and untrained men"* (Acts 4:13) would have made it. We would have opted instead for experienced Pharisees.

The Problem with the Résumé Method

Looking at résumés isn't inherently wrong, but they tell you little of who someone really is, and less of what they will become. One danger is their invitation to focus outwardly rather than inwardly. Consider the résumés of Saul and David.

📖 Look at 1 Samuel 9 and identify Saul's credentials, humanly speaking.

Saul's was great. He came from good stock – the son of a *"mighty man of valor."* He was the best-looking guy in Israel and a foot taller than all the competition (1 Samuel 9:1-2). What his portfolio didn't disclose however, was his selfish pride (see 1 Samuel 15:12), rebellion (see 1 Samuel 15:11, 22-23), jealousy (see 1 Samuel 18:8-9), cowardice (see 1 Samuel 10:21-22; 1 Samuel 17:11), and tendency toward being a people-pleaser (see 1 Samuel 15:24). He was everything Israel wanted in a king, but did they want the right things? They were looking for a strong, visible leader instead of God's choice. Scariest is the reality that God let them have their way. Saul turned out to be a dismal failure (note: Israel having a king is not wrong as seen from Genesis 49:10; Numbers 24:17; and Deuteronomy 17:14-20, but first they must recognize God's Lordship and rule in their lives. Until that happened, a king would not meet their needs).

📖 Look at 1 Samuel 16 and identify David's credentials, humanly speaking.

Consider a second résumé. This baby of a farm family had tended sheep but had no sheepskin hanging on the wall. He fought major battles, but alone with only small towns to talk about. He had a heart after God's heart, but how do you list that in your accomplishments? As a physical specimen he didn't hold a candle to Saul. He didn't even stand out among his own brothers. When Samuel asked to review Jesse's sons, David's own father discounted him as a candidate and left him tending the sheep. But God was able to see past this deficient résumé. You see, such forms record the past, but not the future, and reflect the outside, but not the inside. They may catalog how many fights the person has been in, but not how much fight they have in them.

When God appoints a new king over Israel, we see the right process in action. First, Samuel sees the need and God lays a direction on Samuel's heart (Jesse, the Bethlehemite). Then God has Samuel look at each of Jesse's sons one at a time. When Samuel sees Eliab, the oldest, he thinks, "Here is the one." God corrects Samuel's wrong thinking by saying, *"...man looks at the outward appearance, but the Lord*

Philosophy of Calling Church Staff (Continued)

looks at the heart" (1 Samuel 16:7). It isn't until David is brought before him that Samuel hears God say, "This is the one." What a difference this process produces. With Saul, Israel was looking outwardly, and they got exactly what they asked for. The problem was, they were asking for the wrong thing. With David, Israel got what <u>God</u> was asking for, *"...a man after My heart, who will do all My will."* (Acts 13:22). If a church is asking for the wrong thing, God may just give them a Saul, but soon they will have to start looking again.

Identifying the Process

📖 Let's look more closely at the calling of David and see if we can identify God's process. Read 1 Samuel 15:24—16:13 and write down every principle you observe there about the process of affirming God's calling of a leader.

First, Samuel comes to an awareness of a need. First Samuel 16:1 indicates Samuel is grieving over Saul. He recognizes the need for godly leadership. Even then, however, it takes the revelation of God for him to see that what is needed is a new king. Second, God gives Samuel a direction to look. Notice that it is God who sends Samuel to the family of Jesse (1 Samuel 16:2). Samuel doesn't start looking for the person until he starts looking at God. Third, Samuel looks at Jesse's sons one at a time. He doesn't make a beauty pageant out of it to see who looks best out of the group. He doesn't compare the candidates to each other, but one-by-one places each before God. Notice, Samuel doesn't look at the next candidate until he has heard from God about the one before him. Fourth, Samuel has to start looking for the right things. Samuel has some learning to do, for the Lord has to rebuke him because he is looking for the wrong things. If we are looking for the wrong things, we may find what we are looking for without ever finding what God wants. God's admonition is to look at the heart. We'll address that further in a minute. Recognize the change after the Lord rebukes him about Eliab. No longer are Samuel's eyes looking at the person. Now they are looking to God about the person. The difference is significant. Fifth, it is not Samuel who is calling. When Jesse brings Abinadab before Samuel, his response is, *"Neither has the Lord chosen this one."* It is God who calls, not people. A church does not call a pastor; it merely affirms the Lord's call. When a pastor is called, he is not called to serve a congregation, but to serve <u>the Lord</u> at a particular congregation. This not only shapes the calling process, but also the serving process. Sixth, when Samuel didn't find what he was looking for, he didn't "make do" with the best of what was available. He kept looking until he found God's person (1 Samuel 16:11,12). Seventh, once Samuel knew God's choice, all he had left was to anoint them, and publicly affirm what God had already revealed. He did this in front of David's brothers so that everyone would know that Samuel, the prophet of God, stood behind him.

A Man After God's Own Heart

Clearly what is most important to God in a person is their heart. When a church considers a candidate, the heart is what must catch its attention. Not only is this issue of the heart communicated clearly in the Old Testament, but it is also placed as paramount in the New Testament. Scripture has a lot to say about

SERVANT APPROACH LEADERSHIP TRAINING: Building Biblical Philosophy   (revised 2/20/223)

Philosophy of Calling Church Staff (Continued)

appointing elders (pastors). The criteria for selecting church leaders are extensive, but in each list the focus is not on abilities, but character (see 1 Timothy 3:1-7; Titus 1:6-9). Again, we see that what is inside the person is most important.

📖 Take a few minutes to read through 1 Timothy 3:1–7 and Titus 1:5–9, and identify first of all the technical skills mentioned there for leaders.

Of the two major passages, neither says anything about training except as it relates to the Word of God. First Timothy 3:2 says an elder must be *"able to teach,"* and in Titus 1:9 we are told that one must be able to *"...exhort in sound doctrine and to refute those who contradict."*

📖 Now, take some time to make note of all the character issues mentioned there and their bearing on a person's ability to lead spiritually.

Affirmed By The Sending Church

Up to this point, we have said a lot about the calling church, but where does the sending church come into the picture? Are they simply the losers in this equation? While most churches do not consider this dimension, to God sending is just as important as calling. We see this principle illustrated beautifully at Antioch (Acts 13:1-3). Here we see Barnabas and Saul (Paul) called out by the Holy Spirit to a new work.

📖 Read Acts 13:1–4 and identify to whom the calling of Barnabas and Saul was revealed, and from whom the call came.

The Lord revealed His calling not just to Barnabas and Saul, but to all the leaders at Antioch. The calling of God was affirmed through the sending out of them by the leadership. This supports the common practice of a pastor being ordained by the sending church, not the calling church. Who knows this person better than those where they have been? If God is truly calling a person, then everyone ought to be able to rejoice in the new task, including those the candidate is leaving. Not only does involving the sending church become a safeguard for anything unknown about the person, but it also draws everyone's eyes to God for the transition process. As we look at Paul and Barnabas after this sending out, clearly the relationship with Antioch does not end there (Acts 14:21, 22, 26-28; 15:30-35; 18:22-23). Beware of a person who doesn't want a relationship with the place they are leaving.

SERVANT APPROACH LEADERSHIP TRAINING: Building Biblical Philosophy   (revised 2/20/223)

PHILOSOPHY OF CALLING CHURCH STAFF (CONTINUED)

A Biblical Job Description

Once a person is called by God and this is affirmed by the local body, the job is not finished. We must make certain that they are given a Biblical job description. What does God expect a pastor to do? The one passage where the term "pastor" is used in the New Testament is the most overlooked when it comes time to define the job description. Ephesians 4 is very specific not only about what a pastor is to do, but also what they are not to do.

📖 Look at Ephesians 4:11, 12 and identify the Biblical role for church leadership and for members of the body.

Verses 11 and 12 tell us: *"And He gave some as apostles, and some as prophets, and some as evangelists, and some as pastors and teachers, for the equipping of the saints for the work of service, to the building up of the body of Christ."* A pastor's main job is to equip the saints to be effective in their service to the Lord. It is not a pastor's job to do all the work of service. A church which sees the pastor as the minister and the congregation as spectators will accomplish little for the kingdom. A pastor, more than anything else is called to be an equipper. This is true regardless of the appointed role. A youth pastor needs to equip leaders to minister to the youth. An education pastor needs to spend their time equipping the teachers. All pastors are to be equippers. If they don't equip, they aren't Biblically functioning as pastors regardless of what we call them. How do pastors equip? They equip by ministering the Word. In 2 Timothy 3:17 we see that it is the Word of God which equips us for every good work. We see this priority illustrated beautifully in the first century church. When there was a need for more ministry, the church leaders didn't neglect their primary task in order to meet the need. Instead, they equipped and unleashed the laity. James addresses the need by saying, *"It is not desirable for us to neglect the Word of God in order to serve tables. Therefore, brethren, select from among you seven men of good reputation, full of the Spirit and of wisdom, whom we may put in charge of this task. But we will devote ourselves to prayer, and to the ministry of the Word"* (acts 6:1-7). The result of these right priorities was that *"...the Word of God kept on spreading; and the number of the disciples continued to increase greatly in Jerusalem".*

Wrapping it Up and Taking it Home

Where do we go from here? Whoever are entrusted with the task of looking for a church staff member must understand the dual focus of their role. They are responsible to hear from God, and to communicate with the body what they are hearing from God. The first dimension of their focus is to hear from God. Plurality and unanimity are essential to this. While Samuel was the sole person with the task of calling David, it would not be wise to do it that way today unless there is a prophet in your midst with direct access to God. What God did through individual representatives in the Old Testament, He chooses to do through a plurality in the New Testament. Whether that plurality is a group of elders or a committee, they will answer to the body they serve and to the Lord whom they seek.

Plurality brings accountability to the process and decentralizes power. This group of people will need the strength and sensitivity of each other as they bear the responsibility of hearing God. And they must understand that hearing God is their job. Their task is not to give opinions but to hear God. This is why you want people of spiritual maturity and discernment to make up this group.

This is also why their decision should be unanimous. God will not be saying two different things. If the committee is divided, some or all of them have not heard God yet, or perhaps God has not spoken. The

PHILOSOPHY OF CALLING CHURCH STAFF (CONTINUED)

second dimension of their focus is to communicate what they are hearing to those who entrusted the task to them. The confidence people will have in the outcome of the process will be directly related to how well that process is communicated to them as it plays out. For the process to be most effective, it should be shared as it happens, not just at the end. Below is listed the process of David's call as it would look today. These principles should move this philosophy into the practical realm.

PRINCIPLE #1: GOD SHOWED SAMUEL TO START LOOKING. When God rejected Saul, Samuel grieved, but it took revelation to see it was time for a new king. When a preaching pastor leaves the need is obvious. However, if growth means there ought to be a children's pastor, that need may not be as evident. Sometimes God must show that need, but even that is not enough by itself. Have you looked to God for what is needed (and when)? We want to look to God about everything, but sometimes we get focused on needs and miss opportunities.

PRINCIPLE #2: GOD SHOWED SAMUEL WHERE TO LOOK. Once Samuel saw the need, God sent him to the family of Jesse, the Bethlehemite (1 Samuel 16:2). That ought to be our starting point – to ask God where to look. How can you employ this principle? Pray fervently, asking for divine sensitivity. Look to the Lord about the person before looking for the person. Let God guide you in a direction to look.

PRINCIPLE #3: SAMUEL CONSIDERED THE CANDIDATES ONE AT A TIME. Of all the principles to glean from David's anointing, this is paramount. Samuel didn't gather Jesse's sons together and pick the best one. If he had, he'd have stuck with Eliab, the oldest, and missed God's person. Considering a group, our focus becomes finding the best or most qualified among them, and we turn the whole process into a beauty pageant. Our goal though, is not to find who looks best in a bathing suit.

PRINCIPLE #4: SAMUEL HELD EACH CANDIDATE BEFORE THE LORD. One look at Eliab and Samuel thought *"Surely the Lord's anointed is before Him"* (1 Samuel 16:6). If Samuel leaned on his own understanding, the process would have ended there, but God intervened and redirected. With each son after Eliab, Samuel's answer was *"Neither has the Lord chosen this one"* (see 1 Samuel 16:8,9,10). He held each before the Lord. If we don't want to miss God, we must do this. We can't consider the next candidate until we have heard from God about the present one. Implicit in Samuel's approach was the recognition that it was God's job to call the king. His was to identify and affirm the one God called, and it is ours as well. If Christ is the head of the church, and He says, *"I will build My church,"* (Matthew 16:18) then we better be wary of affirming someone He isn't calling. We better not lean on our logic. Samuel's logic was impressed with Eliab, but David was God's choice.

PRINCIPLE #5: SAMUEL LET GOD CHANGE WHAT HE LOOKED FOR. Samuel almost picked the wrong person by focusing only on outward appearance and the present task. Through his relationship with the Lord, he was redirected in what to look for. David was young, but God saw the future potential of him growing into the role. His heart for God qualified him. Like Samuel, we can put too much stock in externals and undervalue the heart. Skills, training, and experience matter, but I've learned that when a person has a true heart for God, you can always add the training. If the heart isn't there, no amount of training, skill or experience can compensate. We need to consider the heart first, and we need to ask the Lord, "Are we looking for the right things?"

PRINCIPLE #6: SAMUEL CONTINUED UNTIL HE FOUND GOD'S CHOICE. When Jesse was finished, Samuel wasn't. Jesse apparently had already written off David as being too young. Were a church committee in charge of this process they might have been tempted to look at the seven candidates they had seen and settle for the best of the group instead of looking for David. No matter how long the process

Philosophy of Calling Church Staff (Continued)

takes, you have to wait until you hear from God. You may not think you have time to keep looking, but if you get the wrong person, you'll have to make time to start looking again.

PRINCIPLE #7: ONCE HE FOUND GOD'S CHOICE, HE AFFIRMED THEM PUBLICLY. Once Samuel identified David, God had him to anoint him with oil *"...in the midst of his brothers."* It is significant that it was not until he had been anointed by Samuel and publicly affirmed in his new position as king-to-be that *"...the Spirit of the Lord came mightily upon David from that day forward"* (1 Samuel 16:13). I believe there is an important principle here. Once you have found God's choice, be willing to stand firmly behind them and support them publicly. They need this as does everyone else. Don't "waver and wonder." Trust what God has done through the process.

Conclusion

In conclusion, the most important aspect in calling church staff is keeping our eyes on God. If we focus too much on the candidate or the need and lose sight of God, we are prone to mistakes. We must do it God's way, for the world's way won't take us where we want to go. We should continually ask ourselves, "Do we want a Saul, or a David?"

SERVANT APPROACH LEADERSHIP TRAINING: Building Biblical Philosophy   (revised 2/20/223)

Philosophy of Calling Church Staff (Continued)

Notes:

Philosophy of Elders and Deacons

© Copyright 2005 by Eddie Rasnake
You may reproduce this chapter at no charge as long as proper credit is given and no changes are made to the document.

One Head

How is the church of God to be led? ...with Christ as the head! This may sound like a simplistic observation, but I am amazed at how easily it can be overlooked. Many pains and problems are caused by people assuming the role as head in the church instead of allowing Christ His rightful place. If He truly is head of the church, then those in positions of leadership are not to be making decisions but rather, should be following direction. Any human leader is only an under shepherd to the Chief Shepherd. That is why leaders must devote themselves to prayer and the ministry of the Word (hearing from their leader and then passing the orders along).

Two Levels of human leadership under the Head

How does the human leadership structure function with Christ as the head? The elder/deacon structure helps a church let Christ be the Head. In this model, elders are charged with serving by leading, while deacons are charged with leading by serving. Deacons do not make the decisions of the church. They are the leading servants. They set an example for others in personal ministry. Often the deacon body will be a proving ground for future elders. This model is no guarantee of following divine rule, though. An elder board can function as a dictatorship if they follow their own opinions instead of Christ. They can be as a democracy if they follow public opinion instead of what they believe to be God's leading. **To operate in a thoroughly Biblical manner, the components of plurality and unanimity are crucial.** In defense of plurality, the terms "pastor" and "elder" never appear in Scripture in the singular except to describe what one does. Paul called Titus to appoint "*elders* [plural] *in every city* [singular]" (Titus 1:5). It seems clear that the ruling body should be a plurality. Humanly speaking, this gives a healthy check and balance. We see the principles of plurality and unanimity reflected in the statement of James at the Jerusalem council – "*Having become of one mind...*" (Acts 15:25). Any Elder can miss God at a given point, but when all are of one mind, that is the best hope that God has been heard. Hearing God is one of the primary tasks of elders—and then share that direction with others. The only Biblical examples of majority rule are negative ones (c.f. OT - only Caleb and Joshua had the mind of God regarding the Promised Land [Num. 13-14]; NT – the Roman contingent ended in shipwreck when "*the majority*" rejected Paul's advice for the ship to port for winter [Acts 27:12]). Congregational rule gives fleshly believers and unbelievers equal say with the spiritually minded in setting the direction of the church. Biblically operating Eldership places church direction in the hands of the most spiritually minded. So, are pastors elders or deacons? Scripture seems to treat pastor and elder as synonyms. It should be noted that Scripture defines pastoring as the primary function of an Elder. The Bible does not define three levels of human leadership (pastor, deacon, and elder) but two (elder and deacon). All church staff, therefore, function either as an elder or a deacon and should be designated as such.

How did we get here?

The apostle Peter gives us one of the clearest and most concise definitions of Biblical leadership found anywhere in Scripture. But we must realize the leadership structure of the first century church did not start out as clearly defined as this. As we look at the definitions of leadership function in Scripture, we must recognize that the later epistles give far more details and specifics on leadership selection and function

Philosophy of Elders and Deacons (Continued)

than we find in earlier New Testament writings or even in Old Testament passages and principles. In this study we will be using Peter's words as a framework for considering all that Scripture has to say about Biblical leadership structure.

📖 Read 1 Peter 5:1-2.

What title does Peter give the main church leaders?

Why do you think he addresses elders as plural?

What are elders to do according to this passage?

Peter calls church leaders "elders". It is a soundly Biblical term, yet foreign in many churches today. It is not just a church term, but was used in the Old Testament as well, referring to the leadership of Israel. Peter here addresses "elders" (plural), indicating multiple leaders. This pattern is true of the Old Testament practice and holds up throughout the New Testament. Each time church leaders are mentioned in the New Testament, they are referred to in plurality (except when describing what an elder does or referring to a particular person). Peter makes it clear that it is the elders of a church that are given charge by God to shepherd a particular flock. The analogy is not without meaning, for just as an agricultural shepherd would care for, guide, feed and protect a particular group of sheep in conjunction with other shepherds, so too does God intend us, His sheep, to be led.

This seems pretty clear and well defined, but this was one of the later books of the New Testament to be written (about 61 AD). How did church structure get to this point? Let's look at the progression of structure and the concept of elders in Scripture. While one is tempted to begin a search of information on elders in the New Testament, both the concept and the term are rooted in the Old Testament. The term appears 143 times in the Old Testament and is a recognizable part of Jewish life and culture.

📖 One of the first instances of "leadership" or "government" among the people of God is found in Exodus 18:13-26, Numbers 11:14-17 and Deuteronomy 1:9-18.

What is the problem here?

What is the solution?

Though elders existed informally before and there are other Old Testament models of "multiple leadership," in Exodus 18 we see the clearest of the early examples. Moses' father-in-law counseled him to spread out the responsibilities of leadership instead of trying to lead the nation and resolve their conflicts by himself. No one man can meet the needs of everyone. In Numbers 11 God instructs Moses to appoint 70 men out of those who were informally recognized as elders and made them official leaders called elders. God promised, *"I will take of the Spirit that is upon you and will put Him upon them, and they shall bear the burden of the people with you, so that you will not bear it all alone"* Numbers 11:17). Even with the prominence of Moses, there existed a plurality of leadership called elders.

SERVANT APPROACH LEADERSHIP TRAINING: Building Biblical Philosophy (revised 2/20/223)

PHILOSOPHY OF ELDERS AND DEACONS (CONTINUED)

The term "elder" is the dominant title applied to church leaders in the New Testament, appearing some 63 times. This stands in stark contrast to the term "pastor" which appears only once in the New Testament (Ephesians 4:11). Both terms are always used in the plural except when referring to the actions or identity of an individual. In other words, "elder" is a plural office, for leadership is a plural function.

> The first time we see a clear picture of leadership structure after Pentecost (the birth of the church) is in Acts 6:1-7. This is in the context of the first century church, and the leaders of the mother church in Jerusalem. Look at this passage and answer the questions that follow.

What was the problem here, and what was the solution?

How many leaders were there in the main leadership group of the church, and how many levels of leadership do we see mentioned here?

What were the responsibilities of the first leadership group, and of the different, newly formed leadership group?

What was the result of this new leadership structure (v.7)?

Were "the seven" of Acts 6 the first deacons?

It appears that at this point the "twelve" (presumably the eleven original disciples plus Judas' replacement – see Acts 1:15-26) were the only leaders of the church and were trying to do everything. We had a plurality of leaders here, yet some needs were going unmet. It is significant that the problem was identified not by the leaders, but by some of the followers. While the twelve recognized the validity of the need, they also saw that it would be counter-productive for them to personally try to meet it. The twelve (they don't call themselves elders yet) rightly saw that they must devote themselves to *"prayer and the ministry of the Word."* This newly appointed group was given no official title but was to function in a manner consistent with what is later termed a "deacon". The result of restructuring the leadership is that the word kept spreading and the number of followers kept increasing. In other words, because of a healthy leadership structure, the ministry was unhindered. The events of Acts 6 probably occurred somewhere around 33-35 AD.

> What does the word *"deacon"* (Strong's #1249) mean? Look up the word in a Greek dictionary and record your insights.

SERVANT APPROACH LEADERSHIP TRAINING: Building Biblical Philosophy   (revised 2/20/223)

PHILOSOPHY OF ELDERS AND DEACONS (CONTINUED)

Deacons are those who render service (*diakonos*) in the local church. As distinct officers in the local church they are referred to in the plural (*diakonoi*, Philippians 1:1) and are mentioned in addition to elders in 1 Timothy 3:8-13.

- The next reference we have to church leadership in terms of chronology is found in the book of James, written somewhere between 45-50 AD. Look at James 5:14-15 and write what you learn there about church leaders.

Here we see the leaders now have a specific title: elders. It is noteworthy that it took some time to get to this place. A second observation is that the term "elders" is plural, yet church is singular. In other words, a specific church is to have multiple elders. The term church here (*ecclesia*) means "the called-out ones." It was a term used in this era of the local gathering of believers. In this case, the elders are called upon to pray for one who is sick. The addition of forgiveness of sins indicates that the wisdom and discernment of elders would be needed to determine if the sickness was a result of sin.

- In 1 Thessalonians (written about 51 AD) although the term "elder" isn't used, we see some specific instructions about church leaders. Read 1 Thessalonians 5:12-13 and write what you learn there.

In these brief verses we see some specific details of leadership function. The leaders were to "*diligently labor among*" the people. They were to "*have charge*" over them. They were to "*give instruction.*" Presumably this instruction would be the ministry of the Word. Clearly these directives are consistent with what we have seen elsewhere. This passage also reminds the body to "*appreciate*" and "*esteem*" those who lead.

- As we move forward in the first century, we find elders become the norm in church leadership. Look at these passages in Acts and briefly write what you learn.

Acts 14:23 –

Acts 20:17 –

Acts 21:18 –

SERVANT APPROACH LEADERSHIP TRAINING: Building Biblical Philosophy (revised 2/20/223)

PHILOSOPHY OF ELDERS AND DEACONS (CONTINUED)

In Acts 14:23 we see that on the first missionary journey, once churches were established, Paul and Barnabas *"appointed elders for them in every church."* These events occurred somewhere around autumn of 49 AD. In Acts 20:17 we see reference to the *"elders of the church"* at Ephesus. This occurred in the spring of 57 AD. Acts 21:18 speaks of Paul appearing before James and that *"all the elders were present."* As best we can discern, this event occurred in May of 57 AD. By this time "elders" was the dominant term for the main leaders of a church, and a plurality of elders in each place was the practice.

> 📖 The next relevant passage chronologically is First Corinthians, written about 56 AD. In it we are given a glimpse of early worship services. Look at 1 Corinthians 14:29. What was the teaching structure of the early church?

The indication of this passage is that every worship service had 2-3 messages given by different people. Not only was there a plurality of leaders, but also a plurality of speakers. The context here is Paul correcting the disorder and wrong practices of Corinth, and what we read are the specific apostolic instructions for what <u>ought</u> to happen in corporate worship.

> 📖 Moving forward in early church history, the next chronological reference is found in Romans 12:3-8, written about 58 AD. Write down what you see that specifically relates to leadership.

In this passage we see spiritual gifts mentioned, and the point made that the different members of the body have different functions. One function specifically mentioned is *"he who leads"* and the admonition is for them to do that with diligence. The word "leads" there literally means "I stand in front of", and points to the upfront nature of leadership. This passage also makes the point that there are some who are specifically gifted to lead.

By AD 61, the leadership structure of the early church had reached a state of pretty clear definition. In that year four books of the Bible were written that give us a mature view of church structure: Ephesians, Philippians, 1 Timothy, and 1 Peter. Let's look at them.

> 📖 Read the following passages in Ephesians, recording what you learn there about church leadership structure.

1:22-23 –

4:11-16 –

5:23-24 –

SERVANT APPROACH LEADERSHIP TRAINING: Building Biblical Philosophy   (revised 2/20/223)

Philosophy of Elders and Deacons (Continued)

First, we see that God has placed Christ as head over all things. Christ, not a pastor or an elder, is the only true head of the church. In chapter 4 we see that He gave different types of leaders to serve the church and equip it for service. It is worth noting that each of these leadership roles is mentioned in the plural. Verse 15 reiterates that Christ is the head of the church. We see this emphasized yet again in chapter 5. Practically speaking, if Christ is the head of the church, then the church is only led properly when those He places under Him in leadership roles are following His lead. The headship of Christ is crucial for any church to function properly.

📖 Look at Philippians 1:1. What are the two levels of leader mentioned there?

In Philippians 1:1 Paul identifies the leaders of the church as *"overseers and deacons."* The Greek word here for overseers is not the word for elder (*presbuteros*), but the word for bishop (*episkopos*) as it is translated in the KJV. The word for deacons is the same. Paul isn't identifying bishops as an additional level of leadership, but as a synonym for elder, since "elder" is not mentioned here. The term "bishop" is rooted more in the Greek culture, while "elder" is rooted in Hebrew culture. Both mean the same thing. As we read what Paul wrote to his disciple Timothy, who was a leader in the church at Ephesus, we see that a two-tiered leadership structure first hinted at in Acts 6 has come to a place of definition and maturity. It is worth noting that 1 Timothy 3 uses the term *"overseer"* (bishop). In Titus 1:5 and 7 the term is treated as synonymous with "elder."

📖 Read 1 Timothy 3:1-13. List the qualifications. What differences or similarities do you see between the qualifications of elders/overseers and deacons as given in this passage?

OVERSEER	DEACON

SERVANT APPROACH LEADERSHIP TRAINING: Building Biblical Philosophy   (revised 2/20/223)

PHILOSOPHY OF ELDERS AND DEACONS (CONTINUED)

Just as we saw birthed in Acts 6, we see here a two-tiered leadership structure. It has become formalized, and the two are called overseers (elders) and deacons. The words themselves help define their function, for overseers oversee and deacons serve (the meaning of the word *diakonia*). A few significant differences are seen in their qualifications. The main differences are that an elder must aspire to the office (v.1), be able to teach (v.2), and not a new convert (v.6). A deacon must first be tested.

📖 Read 1 Timothy 5:17-22.

What does verse 17 tell you about the functions of an elder?

How are sinning elders to be treated?

What does verse 22 say about the appointment of elders?

In 1 Timothy 5:17 we see that elders "*rule*" (superintend, preside over) the body, and that some of them will lead through preaching and teaching. Though all elders need to be able to teach (3:2), not all will do this on a regular basis. Verse 18 also makes it clear that it is okay for at least some of the elders to be paid. Accusations against an elder are not to be entertained unless substantiated by multiple witnesses, but if an elder is guilty and unrepentant ("*continues in sin*"), he is to be publicly rebuked. A third principle addressed here is that elders must be appointed carefully, for those who appoint them will be credited or blamed for their performance.

📖 In light of all we have considered, look at 1 Peter 5:1-5 and write down what stands out to you about the function of elders.

The church is to be shepherded by a plurality of elders who "*exercise oversight*". They are to do this of their own choice. As we saw in 1 Timothy 3:1, they should be elders only if they "*aspire*" to the office. It is important that we realize this. No one should be an elder who is not burdened for the task. Secondly, it isn't wrong for one to desire the office, so long as it isn't from prideful motives. As we see in 1 Peter 5:5, God is opposed to the proud. Elders are not to "drive" the sheep, lording their leadership over the flock, but to lead by the example of their own lives.

📖 As we consider chronologically the evolution of leadership structure in the church, our last stop is in the book of Titus, written about 65 AD. Read Titus 1:5-9 and write what new things you learn there about elders.

SERVANT APPROACH LEADERSHIP TRAINING: Building Biblical Philosophy   (revised 2/20/223)

PHILOSOPHY OF ELDERS AND DEACONS (CONTINUED)

First, we see that elders are to be "*appointed*". Some authority structure must affirm and position these leaders. They are to be appointed "*in every city*". They are to be men of character and men of sound doctrine, able to handle the Word of God. Not a whole lot is mentioned about what elders are to do. It almost seems that the definition of function is assumed by this time.

We have looked at a lot of different things about elders and deacons, but it has been valuable to see these different passages from the context of chronology. Looked at in such a light, we see that while the earlier Biblical directives were general in nature, as time progressed the instructions became increasingly specific. Perhaps the most noteworthy point is that elders are the main term given to church leaders. It may surprise you to know that the term "pastor" appears in the New Testament only one time (Ephesians 4:11) and there it appears in the plural ("*pastors*"). The word pastor means "shepherd" and scripturally seems to be used primarily to describe what an elder does. This requires relationship first before leadership. It necessitates knowing the condition and needs of the flock. Elders are to lead/oversee the church in...

- **Doctrine** [for example, Acts 15 and Acts 20:28-32],
- **Discipleship** [including both formative and corrective/restorative discipleship or discipline, for example, Hebrews 13:7; 1 Thessalonians. 5:12-14; Matthew 18:15-17; 2 Thessalonians 3:6-16], and in
- **Direction** of ministry [for example, Hebrews 13:17; 1 Cor. 16:15-16]. As leaders govern in this way the members are loved/served and learn how to love/serve.

Where does this leave deacons? In the New Testament there is no organized group or board of deacons constituting a body for leadership. The deacons serve as assistants to the elders/pastors in the work of the ministry and as servants of the various needs of the church. No limit is placed on the time a deacon may serve. This may be determined by the **current needs** in the local body [Project by Project], the **time frame** of those needs [Temporary versus more Permanent/Ongoing needs], and the **extent** of those needs [Some needs are great at first but may soon be taken care of]. It is noteworthy that deacons are to "*first be tested.*" They are not challenged to start doing a task but are affirmed in a place of service where they have already proven valid.

While I am not trying to advocate a complete overhaul of every church on the planet, I hope we are able to look honestly at the Scriptures without feeling the necessity of defending our traditions. Though different churches may use different terminology, the values of plurality of leaders, tiers of leadership, unanimity in decision-making and character requirements for those who lead ought to be principles upon which we all can agree.

PHILOSOPHY OF ELDERS AND DEACONS (CONTINUED)

Notes:

Philosophy of Equipping

© Copyright 1996, 2005 Eddie Rasnake
You may reproduce this chapter at no charge as long as proper credit is given and no changes are made to the document.

The Scriptures clearly reveal the need and the importance of God's people being equipped for life and for service through the body of Christ. That such a need is mentioned, makes it clear that we are to progress in maturity. Just because a believer has a spiritual gift, that does not mean they are ready to use it effectively. Paul exhorted Timothy not *"neglect"* his giftedness (1 Timothy 4:14), but to *"kindle afresh"* those spiritual gifts he possessed (2 Timothy 1:6). The Greek word the latter passage uses means to "fan the flames." Clearly Timothy was to develop his gifts as a steward. How are we equipped for good works?

📖 Read Ephesians 4:11-16. This passage presents one of the clearest statements on equipping found in Scripture.

Who are the equippers?

What is their assignment?

What is the result of being equipped?

📖 The word for "equipping" in verse 12 is *katartismos* (#2677). Its root is *katartizo* (#2675). Look up both words in a Greek dictionary and write their definitions.

The word for "equipped" was used in the Greek language to describe
- a wagon completely outfitted or
- documents completed as directed or
- a boat fully furnished with the necessary oars or
- the mending of a torn net or
- the setting of a broken bone

📖 The root word, **katartizo** is found in the following Scriptures. Take a look at each reference in its context and write what you learn.

♦ Matthew 4:21

♦ Galatians 6:1

♦ Luke 6:40

♦ 1 Corinthians 1:10 and 2 Corinthians 13:11

SERVANT APPROACH LEADERSHIP TRAINING: Building Biblical Philosophy   (revised 2/20/223)

PHILOSOPHY OF EQUIPPING (CONTINUED)

These references have to do with being made fit for a task, being ready so that there is no deficiency in any part. A believer who is equipped is one who is ready and prepared to face a task and carry out that task under the direction of His Lord.

How Does One Become Equipped?

We know that it should be our goal to become equipped to serve, but how does that happen?

📖 Read 2 Timothy 3:14-17 and answer the following questions:

♦ What is the first goal of Scripture in our lives according to verse 15?

♦ Once we have begun a relationship with Christ, how does the Word of God work in our lives for growth (v.16)?

♦ According to verse 17, what is to be the ultimate outcome of Scripture's work in our lives?

♦ Look up the two words translated *"adequate"* and *"equipped"* (NASB) and give their meanings. What do they convey about the Scriptures?

Adequate:

Equipped:

📖 Next, meditate on Hebrews 13:20-21 and make note of what you learn there about the process of being equipped.

It is interesting to notice what weaves together in our lives to equip us for service. In 2 Timothy 3:16-17 we find an additional component. It is the working of the Word of God in our lives that leaves us *"equipped"* for every good work. As we saw earlier, Ephesians 4:11-12 tells us that the Lord has given gifted leaders to the church who are used to equip the laity for works of service. Each of the offices listed in Ephesians 4:11 (apostles, prophets, evangelists, pastors and teachers) have as their primary ministry the communication of the Word of God. Although we can learn much from Scripture that will have an equipping work in our lives, we also need to sit under good teaching of the Word on a regular basis. In Hebrews 13:20-21 we see yet another dimension of this equipping process. There we learn that it is the work of the Lord in our lives which will result in us being equipped for every good work. It is not just one thing which equips a believer for service. It is the weaving together of the labor of leaders, the ministry of the Word, and the sovereign working of God in our lives which moves us toward more effective ministry.

Philosophy of Equipping (Continued)

📖 The word translated "equipped" in 2 Timothy 3:17 is a perfect passive participle. What significance do you discover in its tense and voice?

These words are directly related to *katartismos* ("equipping") in Ephesians 4:12— the foundation passage for equipping in the New Testament. The meaning of these two words conveys the idea that the Godly leader who knows and understands the Scriptures will be "competent because he has been equipped [outfitted, furnished]" (translation by Spiros Zodhiates). Because the leader has been equipped, they are now able to help equip others. But lest we think of ministry as a mechanical process, we must remember that teaching means nothing without the work of the Lord in our lives. The Word of God studied and applied under the direction of the Spirit of God will outfit a person for both walk and work, allowing them to help and equip others along the way.

Second Timothy 3:16 speaks to the issue of training in life. That verse says the Scriptures are profitable for *"training in righteousness."* The word "righteousness" (#1343) has to do with fulfilling what is due to God and to man. In other words, it has to do with right relationships—being, doing, saying, and giving to God and to one another what is right. The Scriptures guide us into those right relationships.

The word for "training" is *paideia* (#3809) and refers to the instruction of children. *"Training in righteousness"* is training in the right God has upon a person. It starts with "realizing God's claims upon us by the miraculous regenerating action of the Holy Spirit." In other words, there is a surrender from the heart to the will and ways of God. This continues in the work of God's Spirit in child-training us in right actions and right attitudes according to God's definition of right (Hebrews 12:1-11). God works through the everyday affairs of life to give us the training opportunities to apply the tool of Scripture—the Word of Life—by the power of the Holy Spirit and thus do what is righteous.

A person who is equipped with the tool of Scripture and being trained in righteousness in daily life is then prepared for the God-given tasks of the Kingdom of God. He or she has the God-given ability and power to walk in the will of God and help others do the same. Second Timothy 3:17 states it simply as being *"adequate, equipped for every good work."* Those "good works" (*agathos*) are works that benefit others and bring glory to God.

What Are the Results of Being Equipped?

📖 What are the *results* of being equipped according to Ephesians 4:11-16?

The measure of how well a local body of believers is equipped is found in the fruit they bear. One of the first evidences of being equipped is that there is unity. What unifies us is the faith. If we all are growing toward the same definition of maturity, then the closer we get to that maturity, the closer we get to each other. As a result, we have doctrinal stability. Believers are not as children in their thinking, nor are they easily swayed by every wind (passing breeze) of doctrine. We are not gullible or easily tricked. As we embrace the truth, not only are we protected from error by that truth, but we also become agents of that truth as we speak it to others. By growing up in Christ, we find where we fit in His body. As we exercise our gifts properly, we become a benefit to all believers and can be used to build them up.

SERVANT APPROACH LEADERSHIP TRAINING: Building Biblical Philosophy   (revised 2/20/223)

Philosophy of Equipping (Continued)

When we live this way people are built up and strengthened in their daily walk with God. They love others more and are loved by fellow members of the body of Christ. Each strengthens and encourages the other. In a nutshell, maturity means ministry. As we are equipped, good works result. When equipping is emphasized and all begin to become ministers, all the needs of the body can be met. In addition, the body is able to have a surplus of ministry so that other places can be touched as well. That is what it means to be a body of equipped saints.

PHILOSOPHY OF EQUIPPING (CONTINUED)

Notes:

Philosophy Student Ministry

© Copyright 2003 David Thompson
Associate Pastor of Youth, Woodland Park Baptist Church
You may reproduce this chapter at no charge as long as proper credit is given and no changes are made to the document.

I. A BIBLICAL PHILOSOPHY OF YOUTH MINISTRY
"Why do we do what we do?"

    A. What was the last command Jesus gave us?

Matthew 28:18-20 - *"Go therefore and MAKE DISCIPLES of all the nations, baptizing them in the name of the Father and of the Son and of the Holy Spirit, teaching them to observe all that I commanded you; and lo, I am with you always, even to the end of the age."*

        1. Jesus' command – "Make Disciples
            >baptize them
            >teach them to obey Jesus

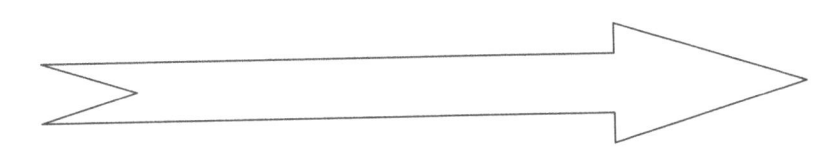

OUR PURPOSE

DISCIPLESHIP

        2. Jesus' promise – "I am with you always"
            >to strengthen you with His Presence
            >to surround you with His Love

Programs don't work…God works. Without faith in God and His power we are wasting our time. Faith is living as though the Bible is true, even when I do not feel it is true.
- 1 Corinthians 2:2-5 - *"For I determined to know nothing among you except Jesus Christ, and Him crucified. And I was with you in weakness and in fear and in much trembling. And my message and my preaching were not in persuasive words of wisdom, but in demonstration of the Spirit and of power, That your faith should not rest on the wisdom of men, but on the power of God."*
- 2 Corinthians 4:7 - *"But we have this treasure in earthen vessels, so that the surpassing greatness of the power will be of God and not from ourselves."*
- Hebrews 11:6 - *"And without faith it is impossible to please Him, for he who comes to God must believe that He is, and that He is a rewarder of those who seek Him."*

    B. Why does the student ministry exist?

        WITH GOD'S POWER - surrendered

            TO MAKE DISCIPLES – as a lifelong learner

                OF JESUS CHRIST – to the LORD, not a program, a person, or a place

SERVANT APPROACH LEADERSHIP TRAINING: Building Biblical Philosophy   (revised 2/20/223)

PHILOSOPHY OF STUDENT MINISTRY (CONTINUED)

C. How do we know that we are Jesus' disciples?

   a. **Disciples abide in the <u>Word</u>** – "the truth shall make you free"
Jesus said in John 8:31-32 - *"If you abide in My Word, then you are truly disciples of Mine: and you shall know the truth, and the truth shall make you free".* Jesus said in John 15:3 - *"You are clean through the Word which I have spoken to you."*

   b. **Disciples abide in His <u>Love</u>** – "love one another"
Jesus said in John 13:34-35 - *"A new commandment I give to you, that you love one another, even as I have loved you, that you also love one another. By this all men will know you are My disciples, if you have love for one another".*

   c. **Disciples abide in the <u>Vine</u>** – "bear much fruit"
Jesus said in John 15:5,8 - *"I am the Vine, you are the branches; he who abides in Me, and I in him, he bears much fruit; for apart from Me you can do nothing. By this is My Father glorified, that you bear much fruit, and so prove to be My disciples".*

II. GOALS IN YOUTH MINISTRY

"What does a healthy youth ministry look like?" *Acts 2:42 - "They were continually devoting themselves to the apostles' teaching and to fellowship, to the breaking of bread and to prayer."*

A. Since discipleship is our purpose of why we exist, what are our goals to accomplish this purpose?

- **The Great Commandment – Matthew 22:37-40**
"You shall love the Lord your God will all heart, and with all your soul, and with all your mind. This is the great and foremost commandment. The second is like it, You shall love your neighbor as yourself. On these two commandments depend the whole Law and the Prophets."

- **The Great Commission – Matthew 28:19-20**
"Go therefore and MAKE DISCIPLES of all the nations, baptizing them in the name of the Father and of the Son and of the Holy Spirit, Teaching them to observe all that I commanded you; and lo, I am with you always, even to the end of the age."

1. "Love the Lord your God with all your heart" is a call to <u>Worship</u>.

2. "Love your neighbor as yourself" is a call to <u>Ministry</u>.

3. "Go and make disciples of all nations" is a call to <u>Evangelism</u>.

4. "Baptizing them" (incorporating them into the body) is a call to <u>Fellowship</u>.

5. "Teaching them to obey" is a call to <u>Training</u>.

OUR GOALS

1. Worship   2. Ministry   3. Evangelism

4. Fellowship   5. Training

SERVANT APPROACH LEADERSHIP TRAINING: Building Biblical Philosophy

PHILOSOPHY OF STUDENT MINISTRY (CONTINUED)

1. Worship – celebrating God's presence and honoring Him with our lifestyles
2. Ministry – demonstrating God's love by meeting the needs of others we love
3. Evangelism – communicating the good news of Jesus Christ with those who don't yet have a personal relationship with Him
4. Fellowship – incorporating God's people into a family where they can be known, cared for, held accountable, and encouraged
5. Training – transforming God's people by His Spirit with His Word

B. **Who are we called to reach?** Every reachable teenager…
- **Community** "the disconnected" – committed to not attending church and living apart from Christ
- **Crowd** "the connected" – committed to attending church and hearing about Christ
- **Congregation** "the downloading" – committed to a small group and having a relationship with Christ and other Christians
- **Committed** "the upgrading" – committed to spiritual habits and growing in Christ
- **Core** "the transmitting" – committed to ministry and serving Christ

Therefore, with every ministry activity we determine who is our <u>Target</u> and what is our <u>Goal</u>.

IV. **How do we reach them and accomplish our purpose?**

2 Timothy 2:2 *"And the things which you have heard from me in the presence of many witnesses, these entrust to faithful men, who will be able to teach others also."*

Jesus' example – He taught and ministered to the multitudes, the 70, the 12, but primarily to 3…Peter, James, and John. Therefore, we minister to all but concentrate on the core ("faithful").

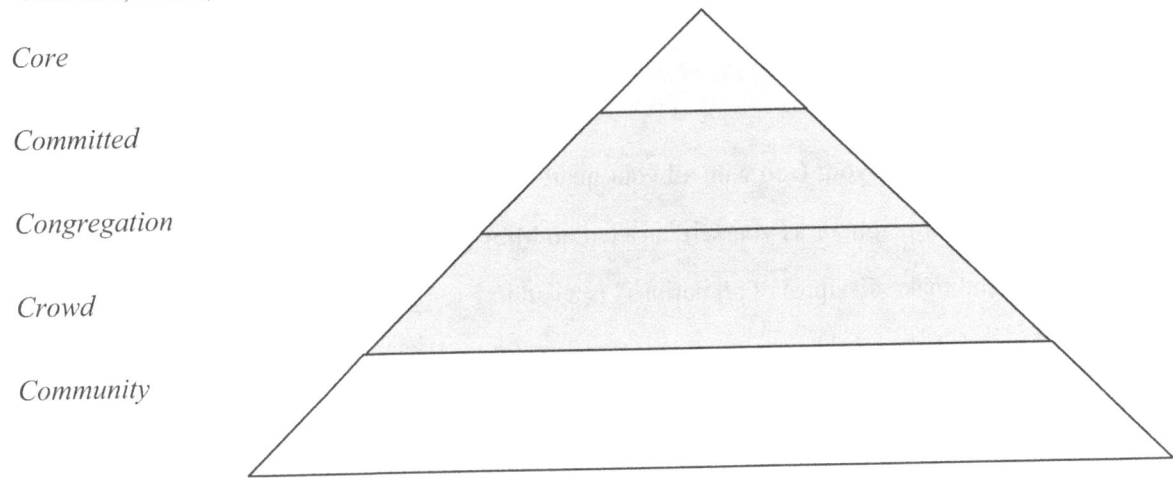

Core

Committed

Congregation

Crowd

Community

Where will you invest your life and ministry? _____

SERVANT APPROACH LEADERSHIP TRAINING: Building Biblical Philosophy (revised 2/20/223)

Philosophy of Student Ministry (Continued)

Notes:

Made in United States
Cleveland, OH
10 January 2025